THEODORE ROOSEVELT'S ARIZONA BOYS

Marty F. Feess

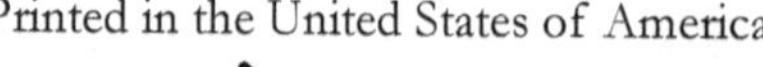

Contents

Acknowledgments

I would like to extend my special thanks to the following people and organizations. At Northern Arizona University, Dr. Philip Rulon was patient, encouraging, and very helpful. Without his help this work would not have been completed. Dr. William Lyon also did much to keep this project on course. Dr. Larry McFarlane, Dr. Earl Shaw, and Dr. David Kitterman also helped me focus this work. My wife, Karen Feess, whose careful eye made her an excellent proofreader, was also indispensable to this project, as well as being patient and understanding through the entire endeavor. Charles Herner, author of *The Arizona Rough Riders*, was very kind to read part of an early version of the manuscript and offer many helpful suggestions. Cynthia Croxen of Flagstaff, Arizona, graciously shared information about her father, Arthur Lewis Perry, who was a trooper in F Troop, wounded at San Juan Heights. In the process of research, I was assisted by many very able and very helpful people at the following facilities: the Sharlot Hall Museum in Prescott, Arizona; the Arizona Historical Society Pioneer Museum and the University of Arizona Libraries Special Collections in Tucson; the Arizona Historical Foundation and special collections of Arizona State University in Tempe, Arizona; the Arizona resource room of the Phoenix Public Library; and the Special Collections and Archives of Northern Arizona University in Flagstaff, Arizona. Any errors in this work are strictly my own.

Introduction

Theodore Roosevelt was not really the first president of the twentieth century. That distinction belongs to William McKinley. But Roosevelt, who assumed the presidency in September 1901, is the perfect symbol of the transition from the nineteenth to the twentieth century. He had a foot firmly planted in each. In many ways TR, America's youngest president, would have been well fitted for the presidency in the late twentieth century with his commitment to activist government, conservation of natural resources, and American leadership on the world stage.[1] He actually reinvented the presidency for the twentieth century as the "bully pulpit" (Roosevelt's own words). But he came of age in the nineteenth, an age of smaller government for a considerably smaller country than America is today. His greatest weakness as president was that he did not seek nor readily accept expert advice. His cabinet members were often used more as functionaries of his own predetermined policies.

Energetic and charismatic, Theodore Roosevelt was also a man of many inconsistencies. Undeniably racist as evidenced in many of his writings, he can be justifiably criticized for failure to take a strong stand against lynching which were common in the South during his tenure. He also made the hasty decision to dishonorably discharge an entire African American regiment from the US Army when the facts of an altercation in Brownsville, Texas, could not be ascertained. Yet Roosevelt,

---

1   Yes, Theodore Roosevelt was the youngest, only forty-two years old when he became president on the assassination of William McKinley. John Kennedy was the youngest man elected president. He was forty-three at the time of his inauguration.

the "square dealer," was also the first American president to entertain an African American dinner guest at the White House. He was then unapologetic and courageously indignant when criticized for the event.[2] One of Roosevelt's most glaring inconsistencies is in part the subject of this book. As a civil service commissioner, Theodore Roosevelt gained a reputation as a crusader for reform, quite willing even to embarrass Benjamin Harrison, the president who had appointed him. President Roosevelt, on the other hand, did not hesitate to reward friends with public office. This was especially true in the territories of the contiguous United States—Arizona, New Mexico, Oklahoma, and the Indian Territory. These territories had been the major staging areas for recruitment into the First Volunteer Cavalry, Roosevelt's Rough Riders of Spanish-American War fame.

While the exploits of the famous cowboy cavalry in Cuba that summer of 1898 are well known, their adventures over the next twenty years are equally fascinating but have been largely ignored. The three Arizona troops had been, in many ways, the heart and soul of the regiment. They were the first three troops enlisted. They provided the regiment with the senior squadron commander (Roosevelt's immediate subordinate), the chaplain, the regimental flag and mascot, and the extraordinary, inspirational Captain Buckey O'Neill. The connection between Roosevelt and the Rough Riders is an essential link to understanding Arizona in the early twentieth century. Roosevelt's involvement with Arizona also illuminates interesting aspects of his character.

This book is about interesting people. It is not a thesis on political science, but rather a true western adventure. It

---

2   That dinner guest was Booker T. Washington. Unfortunately, Washington was never again invited by Roosevelt to dine at the White House nor was any other African American.

begins in February 1898, only days after the explosion of the battleship *Maine* in Havana Harbor.

CHAPTER 1

Rising Stars

Who would not die for a new star on the flag?
—Epitaph of Captain William "Buckey" O'Neill
First United States Volunteer Cavalry
Feb. 2, 1860–July 1, 1898

"Now we drink the soldiers toast—death or a star," proclaimed Arizona's Adjutant General R. Allyn Lewis at a Phoenix banquet on April 27, 1898. In response, a fiery captain rose to his feet. "Who would not die for a star?" was his reply. This impulsive officer was William O'Neill, the former sheriff of Yavapai County, who had recently resigned his position as mayor of Prescott, Arizona, to pursue his star. The charismatic O'Neill was popularly known as "Buckey" around his hometown, Prescott, for his aggressive play at faro in which he would routinely "buck the tiger" (bet his last dollar). The star in which he was most interested was that of statehood for Arizona.

Arizona's star was no doubt on the minds of many who attended that banquet. O'Neill was one of three honored guests, who had organized Arizona troops which would be soon on their way to San Antonio to join Theodore Roosevelt, Leonard Wood, and recruits from the three other territories to form the First United States Volunteer Cavalry which would be known to history as the Rough Riders. The Spanish-American War had just been declared, and they hoped to fight in Cuba. While they were driven by the same righteous indignation about Spanish atrocities and the explosion of the *Maine* that propelled the country into war, these men of the territories were also hungry for statehood.[3] Valor in the pursuit of the interests of the United States would further the legitimacy of their claim to statehood. Arizona had gained a two-month head start on the other territories in recruitment because soon after the *Maine* disaster, Buckey O'Neill joined with his long-time friend James McClintock to recruit cavalrymen in case war should be declared.

The two men had much in common. McClintock was thirty-four years old; O'Neill, thirty-eight. They had both arrived in Phoenix, Arizona, in 1879, and their association together began almost immediately. McClintock came to Phoenix from California at the age of fifteen to join his elder brother Charles who was in the newspaper business. O'Neill decided to come to Arizona to live after touring the frontier territory with a student group. He wrote to the then Territorial Secretary John J. Gosper inquiring about employment. Gosper, who was the principal stockholder in the *Phoenix Herald*, offered the enterprising young man a job as a typesetter for the paper which was managed by Charles McClintock. From there O'Neill became a reporter in Tombstone. He later started his own newspaper, the *Hoof and Horn*, a shrewd enterprise in

---

3   Arizonans had been anxious for statehood since the 1890 census showed that the territory had the requisite population of more than sixty thousand. In 1892, a constitution for the proposed state was written. The United States House of Representatives passed a bill to admit Arizona at that time, but it was held up in committee in the Senate. James McClintock refers to efforts after this time as "the annual statehood bill."

Prescott which appealed for advertising business by offering a reward for the return of any stolen cattle bearing brands advertised in it. This became a springboard to politics for the ambitious Irishman.

O'Neill soon gained a reputation as a man of principle and became very popular in Prescott. He was elected first as county probate judge, then county sheriff, and finally as Prescott mayor. However, despite his popularity locally, he was unsuccessful in his attempts to gain the top elected position in Arizona, that of congressional delegate. He had been a Republican until 1894. Then, unhappy with what he saw as the self-serving nature of both major parties, he became the leading voice of the Populists in Arizona. Opposition to domination by the railroads and sympathy with the oppressed Mormons propelled him into two unsuccessful campaigns for Arizona's representative to Congress. He had also shown some interest in soldiering before the crisis of 1898. He was among the organizers of a militia group in Prescott. This led to his appointment as Arizona's adjutant general for one term in 1889.

O'Neill's friend Jim McClintock was also a newspaper man with more than a passing interest in politics. His education at the Tempe Normal School (now Arizona State University) had led him into teaching, but after a year, probably influenced by his brother, he became a reporter. McClintock was, and remained, an active Republican throughout his life. He participated in the first Republican Party council ever held in Arizona in 1881 and was a long-time member of the territorial (and later, state) committee. Unlike O'Neill, McClintock generally did not seek elected office himself, but he would welcome a federal appointment.

The regiment which O'Neill and McClintock were recruiting was to be led by Alexander O. Brodie, a former regular army officer who was a graduate of the United States Military Academy at West Point. Brodie was probably the best qualified man in the territory for the job, but his life and career had taken some unusual turns. He had first come to Arizona as an army officer fighting the Apaches. Later military service took him to Idaho. In 1877, when his first wife died and his aged mother needed care, he resigned from the army. By the mid-1880s, he was back in Arizona working as a mine developer and mining engineer. In that capacity, he built a massive dam on the Hassayampa River near Prescott. It was 110 feet high, 400 feet across at the top, and 130 feet across at the bottom, and it created a lake two and a half miles long and six miles around in an area where the stream was previously dry part of the year. On February 22, 1890, that dam broke. The resulting flood killed at least eighty-three people. As sheriff of Yavapai County, Buckey O'Neill led a relief party looking for survivors.

The accident was the result of an unusually large amount of rain which had fallen during nine consecutive days and had been preceded by heavy snowfall that winter. Though no fewer than fourteen lawsuits were filed against Brodie's employer, Brodie, himself, was apparently not discredited by the accident. The amount of rain that had fallen was more than anyone could have reasonably predicted, and Brodie had warned his supervisors a year earlier that the spillway needed improvement. Brodie remained popular in Arizona despite the dam disaster. He was commissioned to command the newly formed Arizona National Guard the following year. Then in 1892, he received the Republican nomination for Yavapai County recorder by acclamation and was elected to that post.

What Brodie, O'Neill, and McClintock shared most, beyond their common desire to fight in Cuba, was a common vision for the development of Arizona, a vision rapidly gaining popularity in the southwest. In order to gain a stable population large enough to be considered seriously for statehood, Arizona would need to develop a system for water storage, and the scale of the work necessary might be large enough to require help from the federal government. Alexander Brodie served on the Hydrography Commission of the United States Geological Survey after USGS Director John Wesley Powell strongly recommended that the federal government construct a system of dams throughout the arid southwest.

James McClintock was among those concerned about the instability of the water supply to the newly booming town of Phoenix. By the summer of 1889, the thought of a dam on the Salt River, which runs through that town, had progressed to the point where a committee of three, which included McClintock, ventured into the mountains east of Phoenix and selected a site below the confluence of the Salt River and Tonto Creek.

Beginning in the 1890s, representatives of western states were meeting annually in the National Irrigation Congress to discuss the water storage problem and ways of drawing the attention of the US Congress to that problem. Buckey O'Neill was a central figure in the 1896 NIC held in Phoenix, a meeting also attended by James McClintock. The enthusiastic O'Neill had prepared well for the conference and subsequently appeared disappointed that his fellow delegates did not seem as interested as he to pressure Washington with specific proposals. He chastised his colleagues for inaction, and they in turn resented his brashness. In the spring of 1898, Major Brodie and Captains O'Neill and McClintock were focused on war with Spain, but issues like water for Arizona and statehood were still in their minds and might naturally have come to their lips in casual conversation with such comrades as Theodore Roosevelt.

When war was declared, O'Neill, McClintock, and Brodie had hoped to receive authorization to raise an entire regiment of one thousand men in Arizona. Brodie had petitioned William McKinley to that effect and had enlisted the endorsement of Arizona Governor Myron McCord, an old friend of the President. To their disappointment, the call came for only 170 men from Arizona to be attached to the First Volunteer Cavalry under the command of Colonel Leonard Wood with Lieutenant Colonel Theodore Roosevelt as second in command.

Because of the early initiative, Arizona had the distinction of sending the first contingent of Roosevelt's Rough Riders, and Buckey O'Neill was officially the first Rough Rider sworn in.[4]

Both Wood and Roosevelt lacked experience as regimental commanders. As Assistant Secretary of the Navy, Roosevelt had agitated for war with Spain for some time. When it came, he insisted on participating and was offered the command of a regiment. Having served for several years in the New York National Guard, he was not totally without military experience, but he felt that he would have to learn to command a regiment. He suggested instead that he should go as second in command to his friend Leonard Wood. Wood, a physician, was in the regular army at the time. Roosevelt and Wood had met and become friends recently as Wood was serving as physician to President McKinley. Wood did have limited combat experience and had even won the Congressional Medal of Honor while serving in Arizona during the Apache Wars. Secretary of the Navy John D. Long, Roosevelt's boss, was sure that his assistant had gone crazy. An April 25 entry in Long's journal is often quoted because it turned out to be quite prophetic. Long wrote in his journal that day:

> My assistant Secretary, Roosevelt, is determined upon resigning, in order to go into the army and take part

---

4   Several nicknames were tried by the press at first. Teddy's Terrors was commonly used for a while. The term "Rough Riders" had been used by Roosevelt as early as 1889 in The Winning of the West. William F. "Buffalo Bill" Cody had also used the term in 1893, calling his extravaganza The Congress of Rough Riders of the World. The connection of the term to Roosevelt's regiment supposedly occurred because Roosevelt was quoted as saying that he was going to join some "rough riding fellows" in the west.

in the war…. He has lost his head to this unutterable folly of deserting the post where he is of most service and running off to ride a horse and, probably, brush mosquitoes from his neck in the Florida sands…. He thinks he is following his highest ideal, whereas, in fact, without exception, every one of his friends advises him, he is acting like a fool. And, yet, how absurd all this will sound if, by some turn of fortune, he should accomplish some great thing and strike a very high mark.

Roosevelt remarked that he would have left his wife's deathbed to go fight. In fact, his wife, Edith, was diagnosed with an abdominal tumor in February. A surgeon removed it, but she teetered on the edge of life for two weeks thereafter. By May she was regaining strength, and Theodore was at San Antonio training with his troops.

The whole country seemed to see this war as a great crusade at the time, and that feeling was enthusiastically shared by the Rough Riders and their leaders. Roosevelt would write from aboard the transport ship "it is a great expedition, and I thrill to feel that I am part of it. If we fail, of course we share the fate of all who do fail, but if we are allowed to succeed (for we certainly shall succeed, if allowed) we will have scored the first triumph in what will be a world movement." He went on to observe that the men of the regiment also appeared to feel similarly.

A strong bond would form between the charismatic Roosevelt and his men as they shared hardships, risk, and glory of what they all vaguely believed to be some great cause. Roosevelt had admired the rugged stoicism of western men while ranching in the Dakotas. When tested in battle, Roosevelt's westerners fought bravely while incurring heavy losses in their very first battle which many American newspapers called a "blunder." Later the regiment followed

Roosevelt up a hill into the fire of entrenched Spanish soldiers. He won their respect because he asked no more from his men than he was willing to do himself. He would get them to the front of the battle where some would surely die, but he would, himself, lead the charge.

One humorous incident occurred when Roosevelt was told by a commissary officer that the beans he wanted for his Rough Riders in the field in Cuba were reserved for officers only. The colonel replied that he would require 1,100 pounds of beans for his officers' mess. "Your officers can't eat 1,100 pounds of beans," the clerk replied. "You don't know what appetites my officers have," Roosevelt responded. The young officer then yielded but warned Colonel Roosevelt that the cost might come out of his pay. Roosevelt readily assented to the possibility and later wrote gleefully, "Oh! What a feast we had, and how we enjoyed it."

Roosevelt even put his reputation on the line by defying the secretary of war and the president to draw attention to the problem of epidemic conditions which threatened the entire army after the Spanish had been defeated in Cuba. He called publicly for an immediate evacuation of troops.

Their connections with Roosevelt later paid high dividends for many Rough Riders, especially after their famous colonel became president of the United States. A kind of Rough Rider network developed in Arizona when President Roosevelt appointed Brodie as territorial governor. Many of Roosevelt's biographers have noted that an unusual number of Rough Riders were employed in government service in the southwest. Burton Mossman, first captain of the Arizona Rangers, warned of a "devastating blight of Rough Riders spreading across the west" when he was replaced by Brodie appointee, and former Rough Rider, Tom Rynning.

Many of these appointments were pure patronage, but many were not. Admittedly, Roosevelt and Brodie often provided low level jobs entirely as a reward for service in the regiment. Roosevelt, however, often sought out Rough Riders on whose talent and integrity he could depend. These were, after all, most of the men whom he knew personally in the territories. Among those whose talent Roosevelt developed was young Frank Frantz, who was selected to be the last territorial governor of Oklahoma. At the time of his appointment, Frantz had the distinction of being the youngest governor in the United States.

Other appointees like Brodie and the wandering lawman, Benjamin Daniels, had lost their way in life. Daniels had a strong resume as a law enforcement official, but he had been tried on serious charges at least twice and had been convicted once. To this he added an assortment of questionable activities. His drifting throughout the west was not always by his own choice. Brodie was respected in Arizona, but he had abandoned a military career and sought desperately to revive it somehow. Having resigned his commission, the West Pointer re-enlisted a few years later as a private. That enlistment lasted only a few months when Private Brodie requested dismissal. In 1891, he became the first commander of the Arizona National Guard but resigned within a year. When war with Spain loomed, he jumped at the opportunity to return to active service as an officer. Only one week after the *Maine* exploded, he was busy helping to recruit an Arizona regiment to fight in case of war, and the next week he wrote to President McKinley for authorization of this scheme.

The West Pointer, Alexander Brodie, made a favorable impression on Roosevelt from their very first meeting. The day after his arrival in camp at San Antonio, Roosevelt noted in his diary, "Major Brodie good man." This is followed by negative comments about the other two squadron commanders which are scribbled over. A week later Roosevelt wrote to his good friend Henry Cabot Lodge that Brodie would be a "dandy" senior squadron commander of the regiment.

Both Brodie and Daniels proved themselves in battle and were rewarded with important positions in Arizona when Roosevelt became president. These two men later gained solid and, by many accounts, outstanding reputations in Arizona—Brodie as governor and Daniels as US marshal. And Brodie, with the aid of Roosevelt, was eventually allowed to reenter the regular army as a major, establishing a credible record and retiring as a full colonel. Brodie and Daniels were more than transformed; they had been reborn. These men were possibly the most useful to President Roosevelt. For these reborn public officials, the angel they felt over their shoulder was Roosevelt. They were deeply in his debt. In fairness to Roosevelt and the Rough Riders, we cannot rule out the possibility that many of the Rough Riders may indeed have been, as Roosevelt often contended, superior men, well fit for government service. Before the Arizonans left for training in San Antonio, the authorized strength of the regiment was increased slightly. As a result, two hundred Arizona men would be accepted into Roosevelt's elite cowboy cavalry. But approximately eight hundred men had to be turned away. The physical examination became a critical component of the screening process. "Many of our best cowboy friends had to be dropped on physical grounds," recalled Captain McClintock later. "Too many of them had broken legs or bullet wounds." Many more were, however, able to pass the physical exam, and hard choices had to be made as to who might make the best soldiers. In theory, the abilities to ride and shoot were paramount in the selection, but many who were enlisted were not necessarily the best horsemen or marksmen. We can, therefore, assume that other traits of personality, local reputation, and other intangibles were considered, and those accepted were in some ways considered to be superior prospects to those rejected.

For some Rough Riders, Roosevelt and Brodie had little effect on the direction of their careers. Among the notable Rough Riders who succeed in Arizona wholly on their own were Daniel Hogan, who would be Flagstaff's first directly elected mayor, and John Greenway, who would have a successful career as a mine developer in Minnesota before coming to Arizona in 1910 and gaining fame as the developer of the New Cornelia Mine at Ajo. (Greenway, incidentally, became a close personal friend of Roosevelt.)

The large number of Rough Riders who became law enforcement officials suggests that the skills required for membership in Roosevelt's cavalry may have transferred well to the law enforcement profession in Arizona. To what extent these law enforcement jobs were a matter of patronage is a question worth investigation. Some authors have speculated that patronage was a key factor in the employment of former Rough Riders as Arizona Rangers, especially after Rough Rider Tom Harbo Rynning became ranger captain.

Five Arizona Rough Riders played key roles as Roosevelt men in the territory. As governor Alexander Brodie is perhaps most prominent. John Greenway did not hold any office, appointive or elective, but was an influential political organizer and acted as an intermediary between local Arizona officials and his friend, Theodore Roosevelt. Ben Daniels, perhaps the most interesting figure among Roosevelt's loyal followers, was the only one of this group who had not been an officer in the regiment. He served as US marshal for Arizona, as was mentioned earlier. The other two are J. L. B. Alexander, who became US attorney for Arizona and George Wilcox, who was the court clerk in Tombstone.[5]

---

5   While the position of Tombstone court clerk sounds quite unimportant, the pay was good. As a matter of fact, at one time Wilcox was being considered for governor, but the speculation was that he would refuse the position if it were offered because the pay cut was too severe.

Two other Rough Riders held appointive positions and played important roles in Arizona. Important, but uninvolved in politics, Tom Harbo Rynning was the long-time Captain of the Arizona Rangers. He held that position longer than the other two ranger captains combined. James McClintock, while he did receive an appointment as Phoenix postmaster under Roosevelt and remained influential with his old colonel, remained a mainstream Republican, rather than a member of the Roosevelt wing. Many of these men had bright futures in a variety of government and nongovernment jobs, but in the spring and summer of 1898, they were all cavalry soldiers—all Rough Riders.

CHAPTER 2

The Regiment

Make yourselves as much like regular soldiers as you can in the shortest possible time. If you think of only that you will be thinking exactly of the right thing and you will have enough to think about to keep you busy. If you devote your time and attention to that, the regiment will be a success.

—*Colonel Leonard Wood*
to the First US Volunteer Cavalry

The regimental structure designed by Colonel Wood at San Antonio necessitated four troops in the Arizona squadron. The Arizona Rough Riders originally consisted of only two: A Troop, recruited in the northern part of the territory by Buckey O'Neill, and B Troop, recruited in southern Arizona by McClintock. A third troop, C, was formed by taking recruits from A and B. J. L. B. Alexander, a forty-year-old Democratic lawyer from Phoenix, came to command C Troop as a captain. Troop D from New Mexico Territory was added to the Arizona squadron, as three squadrons of four troops each were set up. Brodie was the logical choice for senior squadron commander by virtue of his training and experience, but he actually received the position through the intercession of Arizona Governor McCord.

"Roosevelt's cowboy cavalry" is known to have been diluted by a number of "eastern dudes" who joined through connections with him, but even among the Arizona troops, the cowboys and ranchers were not half of the recruits. A good many miners also flocked to the colors in Arizona, especially from Bisbee, but also from Globe, Jerome, Prescott, and various other towns. "Cowboy" was, however, the single most commonly listed occupation among the Arizonans and the majority of A Troop did identify themselves as "cowboy" or "rancher."

With each troop authorized only three officers—a captain and two lieutenants, and many well-qualified applicants in the three Arizona troops—room at the top was difficult to find. For example, George Truman, the lone recruit from Pinal County, had been an officer in the Arizona National Guard. He applied for a commission but was refused and served as a private. David Hughes parlayed the same credentials to become a sergeant. C. E. Mills, a mine superintendent, boasted that he did not apply for a commission because he was too good a private. Thomas Grindell, an English professor at the Tempe Normal School who brought several students into the regiment with him, became a sergeant.

Some of the Arizona Rough Riders had been in the army before. Tom Harbo Rynning and William Greenwood had both served in the ranks during the Indian Wars. Greenwood, also called Grandma, admitted to being forty-four years old and had served twenty-three years in the army. Rynning and Greenwood became first sergeants in their respective troops. Rynning was later commissioned a second lieutenant after the creation of C Troop and the transfer of J. L. B. Alexander to command that troop. At least ten other sergeants were veteran soldiers also.

Two of the six lieutenants in Arizona's troops had some active military experience, but experience seems to have been less important than popularity and political skill in these selections. The coveted first lieutenant positions went to Frank Frantz of A Troop, a mining company clerk; George Wilcox of B Troop, a Phoenix farmer who had served in the regular army as a hospital orderly; and C Troop's Robert Patterson, a rancher and banker who had organized the volunteers in Graham County. Selected as second lieutenants were Joshua Carter, a Prescott clerk, A Troop; Rynning, B Troop; and Hal Sayers, a Harvard graduate from a Denver military family who had arrived at San Antonio with Colonel Wood, C Troop. B Troop had elected their officers.[6]

After barely a month of training at San Antonio, the First Volunteer Cavalry entrained for Tampa, Florida. In Tampa, they found what Roosevelt called "a perfect welter of confusion." Because of the confusion caused by lack of planning and preparation, the Rough Riders had an advantage over other volunteer regiments. That advantage was Theodore Roosevelt's determination to get into the fight. In his book, *The Rough Rider*, Roosevelt asserts that at least some of the members of the regiment joined this unit rather than any other because they felt that Roosevelt would get them into the fight.

A bitter disappointment occurred when the Rough Riders learned that, because of severely limited transportation, only two of the three squadrons and only a few of the horses (for the officers) would be allowed to go to Cuba. Dubbed by the adoring press as "Roosevelt's Rough Riders," those still lucky enough to go to war would joke that they had now been reduced to "Wood's Weary Walkers." Arizona's C Troop

---

6   Much of the background information on individual trooper provided in this chapter is from Arizona Rough Riders, the excellent work by Charles Herner.

was left in Tampa along with three other troops to care for the horses.

On the evening of June 7, after several days of waiting in Tampa, the Rough Riders received orders to be at the embarkation docks by dawn the next day. Trains were deployed to haul soldiers the nine miles from camp to the docks. In the confusion at the railroad tracks, the Rough Riders waited while regular army troops entrained. At one point, the Rough Riders were ordered to another track. They went and they waited. Eventually, some drifted away into nearby taverns. According to Roosevelt, he sent out details to locate these men after which the men camped for the night by the tracks. Later that evening, Roosevelt commandeered an empty coal train which was headed in the opposite direction. On his order, that train backed up the entire nine miles to the rendezvous point. After a sooty ride, the Rough Riders arrived just before dawn. The determination of Wood and Roosevelt caused the Rough Riders to hustle ahead of some regular army regiments in the scuffle for transport at the docks. They boarded the first available ship at the first opportunity. That ship was the *Yucatan*. A band aboard kept the troops entertained much of the time. The unofficial regimental theme song was "There'll Be a Hot Time in the Old Town Tonight."

The Rough Riders endured several hot nights off the coast of Florida before an American armada including the *Yucatan* headed for open sea on June 13. According to Roosevelt, none of the Rough Riders, not even he and Wood, were entirely sure of the destination.[7] They would soon have a very hot time in Cuba. As the *Yucatan* began steaming toward the island, Theodore Roosevelt wrote to his sister, Corrine, "Those of us who come out of it safe will be bound together all our lives by a very strong tie."

---

7   Puerto Rico was a possible alternative.

Even before the landing on Cuban soil was completed, Captain O'Neill had distinguished himself for his courage. Two African American soldiers of the Tenth Regular Cavalry were drowned when their landing boat capsized. They were weighted down with heavy equipment. O'Neill, who was at the time standing on the pier where they were to debark, instantly dove into the dangerously stormy water and remained submerged for some time searching for them. He emerged unsuccessful, but Colonel Wood noted the incident and recommended O'Neill for the Medal of Honor.

The only other excitement for the Rough Riders during their first forty-eight hours in Cuba occurred about that same time when Sergeant Albert Wright of Yuma, Arizona, planted the regimental flag and the transport ships saluted it with fifteen minutes of whistles and horns. The landing had been unopposed at Daiquiri about twenty-five miles from Santiago, the military objective. The Spanish had also evacuated Siboney, another coastal town nine miles closer to Santiago. They had chosen their defensive position at Las Guasimas, considerably inland.

The Cuban insurrectos, US allies, closely monitored the movement of Spanish troops. American troops who had landed at Daiquiri on June 22 marched to Siboney the next day to meet troops coming ashore there. The insurrectos assured the Americans that the Spanish were gone from that town. The senior officer at Siboney on that day was the diminutive General Joseph "Fighting Joe" Wheeler, a former Confederate officer whom President McKinley had cajoled to leave his seat in Congress and fight in Cuba to inspire national unity. Wheeler commanded the cavalry (none of which actually had horses) and determined that the cavalry would lead the attack. He met with General Castillo who informed him that the last known forward Spanish position was at the junction of two roads about a mile before the town of Sevilla at a place called

Las Guasimas. The insurrectos had engaged the Spanish there that morning and left one of their own dead on the road.

In the early morning of the twenty-fourth, the Rough Riders began the march to Las Guasimas up a steep trail then along a high ridge. Colonel Wood still commanded the regiment. With only two squadrons in the field now, Roosevelt was charged with command of the second squadron. Brodie, no longer senior squadron commander, remained in command of the first squadron. Regular cavalry troops took a road nearly parallel to the trail taken by the Rough Riders, but their route ran through a valley and was somewhat easier for marching. The thickness of vegetation on all sides made flank guards impossible.

When the Rough Riders arrived at the precise spot identified as the last known Spanish position, they encountered a substantial Spanish force. L Troop of Roosevelt's squadron was in the lead and suffered the greatest casualties. As Brodie's squadron came on the line, O'Neill's A Troop was assigned to the far right, down the hill, away from the center of the action and close to the regulars who were also engaged on the main road. B Troop was kept in reserve; but when L Troop, at the center of the fight, was faltering under heavy fire, B was rushed to their immediate left. Captain McClintock was soon hit three times by rapid fire in the ankle. He lay helpless and in great pain for some time as the battle continued. He was eventually carried back to the aid station. His wound was severe. His service in Cuba was over, and he would walk with a limp for the rest of his life. Major Brodie organized a flanking movement on the left and began its execution when a bullet tore through his wrist and shattered the bone. He continued to fight until he became weak, then he sat down to smoke a cigar. Able to walk back to the aid station on his own, he would not rejoin the regiment until after the war, then as a lieutenant colonel. One Rough Rider, who thought he saw Colonel

Wood shot, panicked and ran back to the rear claiming that the regiment had been annihilated.

Some newspapers reported this false claim. The actual outcome of this battle was a Spanish retreat toward the ridge called San Juan Heights.[8]

An assault on the Heights was made a week later on July 1. By this time fever, which was to be a continual problem, had necessitated a change in command. Colonel Wood was promoted to general and now commanded the brigade, leaving Roosevelt in full command of the Rough Riders.[9] Early in the July 1 battle, some of Roosevelt's troops were pinned down in a sunken road by heavy Spanish fire from a distance too far to allow individual accuracy. But because of the volume of enemy fire and the Spanish practice of firing in volley, some of the men were being hit. To make matters worse, they were ordered not to return fire because one of the regular cavalry regiments had moved in between them and the Spanish. To calm his men, Captain O'Neill walked bravely erect after deploying them in what little cover the sunken road provided. His men pleaded with him to take cover, but he would not. He was shot through the mouth. The bullet exited at the base of his skull, killing him instantly.[10]

This shock paralyzed A Troop temporarily. Lieutenant Frantz, next in command, first rushed to O'Neill's body then

---

8   The Rough Riders had not used flank guards, but this was because the dense vegetation made their use impossible. They also seem to have run into a Spanish ambush, but the encounter was at the precise spot of the last known Spanish position. While the Rough Riders did incur heavy losses in the battle, the Spanish forces retreated from the field. We must conclude that the Rough Riders knew they were marching into a fight at the approximate location where they were attacked. They were not simply the victims of an ambush.

9   At that time Roosevelt was still a lieutenant colonel. He was not promoted to full colonel until near the end of the war when further sickness among his superiors necessitated his promotion to brigade commander.

10   All of the accounts including Roosevelt's account in *The Rough Riders* say that O'Neill was constitutionally opposed to taking cover himself. But it should be noted that both Wood and Roosevelt had unnecessarily exposed themselves during the battle at Las Guasimas.

toward the rear to find a doctor. The command structure broke down and members of the troop either fought as individuals or joined other troops. First Sergeant Davidson and Sergeant Campbell came to command the second platoon. Frantz, however, apparently returned later during the battle to take charge and rally the troops.[11]

In the confusion Private Henry Bardshar, a strapping fellow from Kingman, attached himself to Colonel Roosevelt. He remained as a kind of personal aide to Roosevelt for the duration of the war.

When Roosevelt finally got vague orders to support a general forward movement, he mounted his horse and personally led a charge up Kettle Hill which began what he later called his "crowded hour." He quickly deployed his troops in a skirmish line for the assault then shouted to his first line of troopers, "Well, come on." They did not move from the ground. "What, are you all cowards? Come on!" he yelled angrily.

To that one of the men replied, "We're waiting for you to give the correct military command."

"Oh," said the inexperienced colonel, "Forward march!"

Roosevelt was on horseback, riding back and forth to direct the charge but staying for the most part at the front of his troops. The Rough Rider assault ran through the Negro Ninth Cavalry which was still not advancing.

Some of the elements of the Ninth joined the charge and the Spanish were driven from the forward mogul which the Americans called Kettle Hill.

Having taken the hill, the Rough Riders soon found that they were in as much peril as before, now from intense fire from San Juan Heights. Roosevelt led another charge. Barbed-wire defenses necessitated that he dismount. Now on foot, he

---

11 Roosevelt mentioned in his official report many Rough Riders who showed conspicuous courage or efficiency in battle. He includes Frantz who he says "also did well" in command of his troop.

was a short distance off Kettle Hill charging forward when he noticed that only five of his men were with him. He ordered these five to stay where they were and returned for his regiment which simply had not heard him command them forward. In his excitement the colonel had not passed the order to advance through the chain of command, as would normally be expected, and his weak, shrill voice certainly would have been difficult to hear in the noise and confusion.

The Rough Riders were between the Negro Tenth Cavalry and the First Regular Cavalry as the entire army of 17,000 advanced on San Juan Heights. The contribution of the Rough Riders, a single regiment of six hundred, probably did not make an appreciable difference in the outcome of the battle.

Some would say that the Rough Riders were away from the heaviest fighting and that, in fact, Roosevelt was never really on San Juan Hill at all.[12] But by getting out in front of the entire regiment and leading the charge personally in his part of the line and by being conspicuously the only man on horseback in the initial phase, Roosevelt showed extraordinary personal courage.[13] The symbiotic relationship that this charismatic colonel and his Rough Riders had with the press insured that this small, perhaps unimportant, fragment of the battle would be headline news. General Wood recommended the exuberant colonel for the Medal of Honor and the recommendation was endorsed by division commander Wheeler and theater commander Shafter. The colonel was also generous in his own recommendations for commendations. He recommended seven for the Medal of Honor and at least twenty-eight men

---

12 General Nelson Miles made this claim. The dispute began because the heaviest fighting occurred on the left part of the line on San Juan Ridge. This part of the Ridge, some claimed, was San Juan Hill. The Rough Riders had assaulted the right.

13 Though Roosevelt had led the charge, he was not the first Rough Rider on the ridge. By his own account several of the younger men who could run faster beat him to the top. Roosevelt was also criticized by the Hearst newspapers for shooting a fleeing Spanish soldier in the back. He did not, however, feel any moral dilemma over the killing.

for various commendations, including Lieutenant Frantz, who had been so bewildered when Captain O'Neill was killed. Frantz was promoted to captain to replace O'Neill while Second Lieutenant John C. Greenway was promoted to first lieutenant and transferred to A Troop.

The remains of Bucky O'Neill were buried in Cuba, but after the war they were exhumed and given a more proper resting place in Arlington National Cemetery. His epitaph reads, "Who would not die for a star in the Flag?" That star would be slow to rise, but through their actions in Cuba, the Arizona Rough Riders won the goodwill and assistance of Theodore Roosevelt in their star quest.

With the capture of San Juan Heights, the main body of Spanish troops was under siege at Santiago. The Americans repulsed a counterattack on July 2. No more serious fighting occurred thereafter. However, Spanish snipers were operating behind American lines. To deal with this problem, Roosevelt selected a detail of approximately thirty skilled marksmen to lie all day in the tall brush to spot and kill snipers. Often heading this detail was the former Dodge City deputy marshal, Ben Daniels, who endeared himself to Roosevelt through his bravery, willingness to hard work, and devotion to duty.

On July 15, the Spanish garrison surrendered, which also ended the sniper threat, but did not end the real danger in Cuba. The Rough Riders' new and very dangerous enemy was jungle fever in various forms. Colonel Roosevelt insisted that the men be evacuated from Cuba at once. With the Spanish surrender there was no need to keep a large number of troops in Cuba he argued. The threat of yellow fever along with outbreaks of malaria, dengue fever, and dysentery made evacuation a practical necessity. The army was slow to respond, so Roosevelt authored a round-robin letter to General Shafter demanding evacuation. Several generals joined Colonel Roosevelt in signing the letter, and it was leaked to the press. (Roosevelt had already provided the press with a copy of his individual letter to Shafter.) After the war, Roosevelt was incensed that he was not awarded his Medal of Honor. He pursued a letter writing campaign to gain endorsement for his medal, but in the end was granted only the consolation prize of a brevet promotion for valor to general. He always believed that he had been denied the medal because of the round-robin letter.

While the bulk of the Rough Riders were in Cuba, the squadron remaining in Florida was having a difficult time of its own. Fever was also epidemic among these troops, and discipline was difficult to maintain, especially as the squadron lost hope of joining the rest in Cuba. Captain Joseph L. B. Alexander, commanding C Troop, even had some trouble with his noncommissioned officers. On June 25, he preferred charges against Sergeant A. R. Perry for "willfully abandoning his post of duty" and being "absent without leave." Perry was allowed to resign six weeks later. Two corporals were reduced to private. And one private who had disobeyed a direct order added "disrespect for a superior officer" to the charges against him by cursing the captain as he was physically being carried away to the guardhouse. And the morale problem in Florida was not unique to C Troop. One of the New Mexico men summed up his feelings by saying, "Tampa was a hell-hole. We were there waiting, thinking we would get over to Cuba, or maybe to Puerto Rico, and nothing happened. A lot of us got sick and a lot got in trouble in Tampa. No wonder. We were there over two months with nothing to do but get sick and get mad."[14]

On August 7, Colonel Roosevelt and the Rough Riders left Cuba for the United States. General Wood remained in Cuba as military governor. The Rough Riders arrived at Montauk Point, Long Island on August 14, the day that the

---

14 Frank Brito quoted in Dale L. Walker, *The Boys of '98: Theodore Roosevelt and the Rough Riders*, (New York: Tom Doherty Association, 1998): 258.

armistice was declared between the United States and Spain. They were met by those Rough Riders who had been left in Florida and Alexander Brodie, now a lieutenant colonel wearing his arm in a sling. A quarantine station was established at Montauk Point because many of the returning troopers were still suffering from some form of jungle fever. On August 19, a more permanent post was established for all the returning troops at Camp Wikoff, also on Long Island.

At Camp Wikoff the Rough Riders continued to command attention. They entertained the entire camp with organized displays of horsemanship. The men also regaled fellow patrons in New York saloons with stories of the war. The highlight at Camp Wikoff occurred on September 13 when the men of the regiment presented Colonel Roosevelt with a bronze reproduction of Frederick Remington's *Bronco Buster*, which thereafter remained one of his most valued possessions. Roosevelt then made a short speech expressing his pride in the regiment and acknowledging the contributions of the Negro Ninth and Tenth Cavalry, some of whom had gathered at a distance attracted by the festivities. After this, the entire regiment filed by at Roosevelt's request so that he could shake hands and say a few words to each man.

Two days later the regiment was mustered out of existence. In addition to his regular pay, the government gave each of the westerners approximately $200 for the trip home. Some Rough Riders were apparently so anxious to get home that they did not even wait to be officially mustered out. As a result, the army was still trying to find several Rough Riders two months later to give them their final pay. Many, however, did not leave the east coast for some time and others squandered their money. Roosevelt ended up buying a great many one-way tickets west for his men.

Although the Arizona men, whom Roosevelt called "the backbone of the regiment," returned with pride, many had served at a considerable personal cost. Most faced uncertainty but also probably felt that their comradeship might help sustain them, not knowing the extraordinary power that their colonel would soon have. Many were still feeling the effects of fever and would have periodic relapses for years. Some would die young from a general breakdown of health resulting from sickness in Cuba or Florida. Roosevelt had stated in his August 3 letter to General Shafter that the health of the army in Cuba was such that "Not twenty per cent are fit for active work." Of the 771 Americans who died in the Cuban campaign, 514 had died from disease.

The Rough Riders constituted an extraordinary assemblage of individuals and an incredible example of the promise of democracy. Aristocrats mixed with cowboys, business leaders, miners, and politicians. Though upper-class men dominated the ranks of major and captain, most of these men were not wealthy, and members of every socioeconomic group could be found in all the ranks from private to lieutenant. Racially, they were Anglos, Hispanics, Native Americans, and men of mixed heritage. Though recruited primarily in the southwest and northeast, their numbers included men from every part of the country. One man had served in the Confederate army.

"T'was a noble bunch of men," reflected Sergeant Cornelius Cronin years later, "including as it did men of every class, creed, and—I almost said race." The Rough Riders did not, of course, include blacks since the United States army was still, at that time, officially segregated. But the Negro Ninth and Tenth Cavalry did charge up San Juan Heights in close proximity to the Rough Riders. During the fighting, black soldiers became mixed with the Rough Riders. According to Roosevelt, a camaraderie between the Rough Riders and the "buffalo soldiers" resulted, and at least one Rough Rider said that these new friends could drink out of his canteen anytime.

There were also several foreign-born Rough Riders. Trumpeter Emilio Cassi, an Arizona resident at the time of his enlistment, was from Monaco and had served in both the Italian and French armies. Sergeant Christian Madsen, from Denmark, had served in the Danish army, the French Foreign Legion, and the French army. He had been wounded and captured in the Franco-Prussia War. After all this, he came to the United States and served fifteen years in the army of the west. Scotsman Robert M. Ferguson, close friend and business partner of Roosevelt, had been a lieutenant in the British army and achieved the same rank in the Rough Riders.

More diverse still was the mass of men who assaulted San Juan Heights. The true America of the twentieth century emerged for the first time that July 1. John J. Pershing, then a young lieutenant with the Negro Tenth Cavalry, recognized the historical importance of that charge when he wrote, "White regiments, black regiments, Regulars and Rough Riders, representing the young manhood of the North and the South, fought shoulder to shoulder, unmindful of race or color…mindful only of their common duty as Americans."[15] Roosevelt, attached as he was to the racial views of his time, could not have anticipated the America which exists today. But he and his Rough Riders had a roll in its inception.

The democracy of the Rough Riders was conducive to camaraderie. After the war, the men wanted to keep in touch with each other. To facilitate their friendships, they formed an association and planned to have regular reunions. Roosevelt became a father figure to many, if not most, of the men in the regiment. Many wanted to assist him in any way possible and still more turned to him for assistance. Some members of the regiment stayed in New York to help with Roosevelt's

---

15 Quoted in Paul Andrew Hutton's "T.R. takes Charge," *American History*, vol. 33 (August 1998): 64.

gubernatorial campaign that autumn. Some had political aspirations of their own at home.

gubernatorial campaign that autumn. Some had political aspirations of their own at home.

CHAPTER 3

Homecoming, 1898–1901

I have played it in bull luck this summer. First, to get into the war; then to get out of it; then to get elected. I have worked hard all my life, and have never been particularly lucky, but this summer I was lucky, and I am enjoying it to the full. I know perfectly well that luck will not continue, and it is not necessary that it should. I am more than content to be the governor of New York, and shall not care if I hold another office; and I am very proud of my regiment, which was really a noteworthy volunteer organization.

—Theodore Roosevelt
November 25, 1898

The Rough Riders strengthened the bonds among the regiment with annual reunions in the years immediately after the war, but they did not immediately become prominent in Arizona politics. Most of those who ran for office in 1898 were unsuccessful, and Roosevelt's power to help the members of his former regiment through recommendations was limited at first. The Colonel, himself, had a political battle ahead that autumn for which he enlisted the help of many of his Rough Riders. Those from the Arizona troops who played a major part in Roosevelt's 1898 gubernatorial campaign in New York were Colors Sergeant Albert Wright and bugler Emilio Cassi.

Roosevelt's status as a war hero had earned him the Republican nomination that year. In his autobiography, he suggests that discussions about his possible candidacy began when Lemuel Ely Quigg, state Republican chairman, visited him at the Rough Rider encampment on Long Island in mid-August. Roosevelt's own letters, however, show that party leaders broached the subject at least by late July while the Rough Riders were still in Cuba. In fact, New York had been buzzing with talk about Roosevelt's candidacy all through July. The *Times* reported on the thirteenth that "Roosevelt for governor" campaign buttons were "widely circulated among organization Republicans." And one Rough Rider private wrote home from Cuba on August 4 that "Rosy is trying to get us back so he can run for Governor in New York."[16]

Under normal conditions party bosses would not have chosen Roosevelt for the nomination. As a civil service commissioner, he had embarrassed the Harrison administration, which had appointed him. Later as New York City police commissioner, he insisted on enforcing the Sunday closure of saloons though his predecessors had ignored that law to avoid conflict. TR was stubborn and independent, not a good team politician. However, the party needed him in 1898. He had a reputation as incorruptible, and he was then a popular celebrity.

The then governor of New York, Republican Frank Black, was mired in charges of corruption related to contracts involved in rebuilding the Erie Canal. As a consequence, the

---

16 Herner, Charles. *The Arizona Rough Riders*. (Tucson: The University of Arizona Press, 1970): 175.

party leaders considered Black unelectable for another term. But whomever the party nominated would be in the tenuous position of defending Governor Black, or at least running with the baggage of Black's record. Perhaps no other Republican in the state could have generated the appeal which Roosevelt had under the circumstances. He had abandoned a prestigious position to face grave danger serving his country in a popular war. His courage at San Juan Heights had already begun to enter American mythology as an ideal of the American character and it was still fresh in the minds of all. In short, Teddy was larger than life. Even party boss Thomas Platt came to the conclusion, however reluctantly, that the Rough Rider colonel was the only viable Republican candidate for New York governor in 1898.

The campaign was launched at a meeting at Carnegie Hall on October 5, which ratified the choice of the earlier Republican convention at Saratoga. In a unique gathering, Republican machine men met with reformers, who had hesitated to work with the machine until then. Joseph Choate spoke of Roosevelt as "the missing link" which now united the "regulars" and the "volunteers." And one of Mr. Choate's fellow volunteers, Dr. Seth Low, president of Columbia University, sent the audience into more than ten minutes of cheers, shouts, and laughter by saying, "It is true that both Col. Roosevelt and Mr. Crocker [Tammany Hall boss Richard Crocker] spent most of last summer on an island, but Col. Roosevelt rode his own horse." A number of Rough Riders were in attendance seated conspicuously on the platform behind the speakers.

The early strategy which Colonel Roosevelt employed played up his status as a war hero and used a substantial number of Rough Riders on the campaign. Typically, uniformed Rough Riders would be seated on the stage where their colonel spoke, or they would enter rallies at precisely planned times. Bugler Cassi would summon the audience to the back of Roosevelt's train during a whistle stop campaign. Roosevelt spoke with pride of his adventures and of his men and was frequently interrupted by cheers and applause nearly everywhere. Rough Riders also journeyed on their own into the New York countryside. Two men of the Arizona troop were the "star attractions" at the state fair. Sergeant Wright, a Democrat from Yuma, explained that he did not speak about politics there, "But you can't tell about the fight at Santiago without mentioning Col. Roosevelt. Every time we said anything about him the crowd went wild."

Many Rough Riders participated in the campaign. Mason Mitchell, a New York actor, volunteered his services, offering to cancel all his theatrical engagements until after the campaign. (He had recently returned from Chicago, where he had been earning more than $500 a week lecturing about his former regiment.) He and fellow actor Buck Taylor of New Mexico used tongue-in-cheek humor to excite the crowds and lure Democratic newspapers into extensive discussion of Roosevelt's record. Mitchell was quoted as saying, "And then out of the woods darted the Colonel with a revolver in each hand and waving his sword in the air he shouted 'Come on boys'...."[17] But the most widely quoted gem of the campaign was this from Taylor:

> I want to talk to you about mah Colonel. He kept ev'y promise he made to us and he will to you. When he took us to Cuba he told us...we would have to lie out in the trenches with the riffle bullets climbing over us, and we done it.... He told us we might meet wounds and death and we done it, but he was thar in the midst of us, and when it came to the great day he

---

17 G. Wallace Chessman, *Governor Theodore Roosevelt: The Albany Apprenticeship, 1898-1900*, (Cambridge: Harvard University Press, 1965): 63-64.

—

led us up San Juan Hill like sheep to the slaughter and so he will lead you. [18]

According to Roosevelt, Taylor's comment "delighted the crowd, and as far as I could tell did me nothing but good."

Other Rough Riders who traveled extensively on the campaign with Roosevelt were Sherman Bell from Colorado and G. Roland Fortescue of New York City. Bell had refused to go to the hospital to get treatment for a ruptured hernia because it would take him out of the war. Fortescue, a young relative in whom Roosevelt had great pride, was wounded during the San Juan charge but continued to fight. The two Arizonans, Wright and Cassi were both prominent in the campaign. Cassi's role as bugler has already been mentioned. Colors Sergeant Wright had planted that first American flag in Cuba, a fact Roosevelt delighted in mentioning as he introduced Wright at rallies.

The Roosevelt campaign exploited the Rough Rider image shamelessly. The colonel approved a plan to have a Rough Rider stagecoach travel through the New York countryside to Buffalo. It would be pulled by eight original Rough Rider horses with three uniformed Rough Riders inside, accompanied by a brass band and campaign speakers. And at one rally 250 "Roosevelt Volunteer Campaign Rough Riders" of German American descent marched in uniforms made to resemble those of the real Rough Riders.[19] This was only one of several rallies which included supporters in Rough Rider costume. The New York *Times* was highly critical of the exploitation. One *Times* editorial said in part:

Whatever else may be, neither the war in Cuba nor the gallantry and efficiency of Col. Roosevelt or of his

---

18 Ibid., 64.

19 Roosevelt was desperate to gain a portion of the German American vote because this element was heavily anti-Roosevelt owing to his strict enforcement of the law closing their saloons on Sundays while he was police commissioner.

regiment is in question in this canvass. The extreme use of men in khakis, as part of the stage setting for Col. Roosevelt's speeches, implies the contrary. It is an assumption that the voters will refrain from supporting the Colonel because of his relations with the Platt machine, or because he professes inexcusable ignorance as to the existence of canal frauds....

Roosevelt's strategy did not work well. He was discouraged until late in the campaign, when Tammany boss Crocker provided him with an effective issue by denying New York Supreme Court Justice Joseph F. Daly renomination, objecting publicly to Daly's political independence. Daly had sat on the bench for twenty-eight years. Roosevelt hammered on the issue of the importance of an independent judiciary. The Rough Rider strategy also continued until the end. The colonel won by the narrow margin of only 17,794 votes out of 1.3 million cast, despite the bipartisan appeal of the judicial issue.

Perhaps Roosevelt's strategy worked best for him because he was a known commodity in New York, especially in New York City where he had been police commissioner.

The anti-Roosevelt *Times* also published many letters to the editor during the campaign which were critical of the paper for their attacks on Roosevelt.

One such letter reads:

The public knows Roosevelt. What has been done by former executive officers in the State has nothing to do with the "colonel." He can be relied upon to enforce the law without fear or favor.... Go after Platt and the rest of the gang, but take it easy on Roosevelt. He's made of the right stuff, has a courage not to be daunted, is a man of the people and will be the best Governor New York ever had....

While Roosevelt ran for governor of New York, his friend and former immediate subordinate, Colonel Alexander Brodie, aspired to the seat of Arizona's delegate to the US House of Representatives. Just as Roosevelt was considered the only Republican capable of being elected New York governor, Brodie represented the best outside hope of Arizona's minority Republican Party to gain the most prestigious elected office in the territory. Of Arizona's twelve elections for congressional delegate since 1874, Democrats had won eleven. The only Republican congressional victory in Arizona during that time came in 1894 when Buckey O'Neill ran a strong third as the Populist candidate, splitting the vote in favor of the Republicans. Republicans could take some heart in this 1898 election not only because they had a strong candidate, but also because the popular Democratic incumbent, Marcus Smith, who had won five of the six most recent contests, was not a candidate this year.

Colonel Brodie traveled widely and ran an effective campaign. Like Roosevelt, he was well received and cheered everywhere he went. He remained dignified throughout the campaign and refused to attack his opponent. His traveling companions were not generally Rough Riders, but rather Arizona Republican dignitaries. Rough Riders were prominent at only one Brodie rally; that was in Phoenix. Brodie did, however, secure the endorsement of at least two former Rough Riders who were prominent Democrats, J. L. B. Alexander and Frank Frantz. Alexander was at first expected to campaign actively for Brodie, but business took him away from Arizona (and a potentially embarrassing commitment) at the time.

The Brodie campaign emphasized the hope of statehood for Arizona but ignored the important silver issue. Democrat John F. Wilson campaigned on the issue of free coinage of silver. Shortly before the election the *Arizona Republican* had predicted Brodie to be a certain winner. But in fact, he was defeated. At least one author has suggested that Brodie's defeat may have been in some way attributable to the resentment of some eight hundred potential Rough Riders turned away from enlistment because Arizona's quota was limited.[20]

However, Democratic victory was normal in Arizona congressional elections in those years, and by not addressing the silver issue, Colonel Brodie appeared to oppose the free coinage of silver. The silver issue was important in 1898 because the 1893 repeal of the Sherman Silver Purchase Act depressed mining, Arizona's leading industry. The Democratic pledge to work for silver coinage may have had more practical appeal than the hope of statehood. Statehood, itself, did not have universal support in Arizona. The Mormons, potentially a significant voting bloc in Arizona then, and generally Democratic, were opposed to statehood at that time. Years later one of Brodie's closest associates recalled the defeat matter-of-factly and expressed pride in that the vote was relatively close.

Evidence also supports the belief that an anti-Rough Rider backlash did, in fact, occur. Approximately one thousand Arizonans were eventually accepted as volunteers for the war. The governor of the territory, Myron McCord, resigned to lead a squadron personally, but it never got out of the country. Other Arizonans did see combat, but reporters singled out only the Rough Riders for glory. The Arizona National Guard, which was conspicuously left out, had opposed the enlistment of volunteers in the territory while it had not been activated. Six Rough Riders are known to have run for office in Arizona in 1898. All were defeated.

Brodie, like Roosevelt, had been thrust forward as a war hero. The Republican Party of New York and Arizona had embraced their currently fashionable favorite sons and in doing so elevated these men from the status of current (and

---

20 Herner, 218.

temporary) war hero to fully participating members in the party leadership. Incompatible ideologies were ignored for political expediency. The old party leaders of both New York and Arizona would later have cause to regret the compromise.

Of the five other Rough Riders who were also unsuccessful in their attempts to launch a political career in 1898, four were Republican nominees. Captain James McClintock ran for a position on the Phoenix City Council. Lieutenant Samuel Greenwald, who had gained his commission for gallantry under fire, was picked by the party for probate judge. Corporal George J. McCabe, who had earlier run for Cochise County sheriff as a Populist, was now seeking that position as a member of the GOP. And Sergeant Thomas Grindell, the English professor, hoped to be Superintendent of Schools for Maricopa County. Grindell made the best showing of the four, being very narrowly defeated. Neither he, McClintock, nor Greenwald campaigned actively. McClintock was still recovering from his severe wounds and remained in an eastern hospital until after the election. Grindell was fighting reoccurrences of fever contracted in Florida. And Greenwald, for some unknown reason, did not return to Arizona until just before the election.

Unlike their Republican opposition, the Democratic Party of Arizona does not appear to have actively sought Rough Riders as candidates for the 1898 election. George Wilcox ran unsuccessfully for a seat in the territorial legislature despite the popular platform of free silver. His unanimous election as a lieutenant of B Troop indicates that he was a natural leader and popular in southern Arizona. His defeat in 1898 supports the possibility of a backlash against the Rough Riders. He proved later that his interest in politics was long-term. The citizens of Bisbee elected him as justice of the peace in 1900 and he became a central figure of the Progressive Party in Arizona in 1914.

Other Rough Riders settled for jobs that would keep them in touch with politics. George Truman applied for a position as a low-level clerk with the Arizona legislature and was at first rejected by a 13 to 11 vote, but by 1901 he and fellow Rough Rider Sol Drachman were both serving as legislative clerks. Thomas Grindell clerked in the Arizona Supreme Court.

The Rough Riders were the celebrity idols of 1898. Unfortunately for them, though, avenues through which that celebrity could be redeemed for success in civilian life at that time were limited, though a New York manufacturer was turning out "Captain Buckey O'Neill" cigars. For Buffalo Bill Cody, the Rough Riders offered potential for exciting, renewed interest in his show which had always included reenactments of famous battles. He updated the show to include a reenactment of the Battle of San Juan Hill with himself as Roosevelt. Over the next several years no fewer than sixteen former Rough Riders, mostly from Oklahoma and the Indian Territory, participated in the reenactment.

Many of the Rough Riders found military life agreeable and some of those who had been left in Tampa were naturally disappointed in the lack of combat experience and were anxious to redeem themselves. Within three months after their separation from military service, New York Rough Riders Corporal Charles Knoblauch and Sergeant John Worden, both of K troop, were reported to be "on their way to Europe in hope of finding war."[21] America soon had a war to occupy such restless martial spirits and many Rough Riders enlisted to fight. The enemy was the Philippine insurrectos.

Rough Rider Captain Maximilian Luna was again commissioned. His first task was to recruit in his home territory of New Mexico and in neighboring Arizona for the newly

---

21   Rough Rider Captain Robert H. Bruce and Major Henry B. Hersey did find a war in Asia a few years later. They attempted to organize a unit from among the veteran Rough Riders to fight for Japan against Russia in 1904.

—

forming Thirty-fourth Volunteer Infantry. James McClintock agreed to help in the recruitment, though he would not (and probably could not because of his injury) go back into the army. Eight Arizona Rough Riders are known to have joined the Thirty-fourth and one other enlisted in another unit.

With the Philippine insurrection and the expansion of the army came new opportunities for commissions. Brodie tried to get back into the army and his former commander supported the effort, but without success. Roosevelt did, however, obtain a second lieutenant commission for young Fred Bugbee who, as a private in A Troop, had refused to leave the battlefield at San Juan after acquiring a gruesome looking head wound. Roosevelt also secured a captaincy for William Dame, who had impressed the colonel with his coolness under fire at Las Guasimas as a second lieutenant in F Troop.

Asked by Secretary of War Elihu Root to recommend candidates for commission in August 1899, Roosevelt named several Rough Riders who showed no interest in reentering the army, but his list is interesting. Recommended most highly were men who would become important political allies. The "best man" among the Arizonans, said Roosevelt, "would be George Wilcox…. Next to him," Roosevelt continued, "Frank Frantz…. I should only appoint him to a lieutenancy, however." This comment about Frantz probably stems from his initial panic at the death of O'Neill, but it is very interesting in light of responsibilities with which Roosevelt eventually entrusted Frantz. Roosevelt's list also included George Curry of New Mexico whom he praised as "among the best officers in the regiment" and a man "who can be depended upon, especially in any emergency" though Curry did not get to Cuba. Roosevelt also had high praise for Mason Mitchell, the actor who had volunteered to work full-time on the gubernatorial campaign, and the Ivy League men, Woodbury Kane, David Goodrich, and John Greenway, though he was sure these last three would not accept a commission.

As Roosevelt began his gubernatorial term, members of his old command deluged him with requests for help. He expressed his frustration and his genuine desire to help in a letter dated January 17, 1899:

> The hard thing is, when one is fortunate above the friends for whom one cares who are not as fortunate. Do you know the Russian proverb: "Once in ten years you can help a man"? It is not oftener than once in ten years that the power on the one side and the need on the other come together…. Of course, in each case the beneficiary had to do the work. All that the other man could do was give the chance….
>
> There are now literally hundreds of my comrades in arms, not only in my regiment, but in the Regular regiments, each of whom thinks I may be able to aid him, and each of whom I would like to help; yet all that I have succeeded in doing is to help a little, in some way, a few. I still hope I will be able to help at least one or two in more substantial ways by getting them the rank they want, the position for which they hope, or the start in life they desire; but I cannot do it for all, and I know that some of them who do not quite understand are unable to help feeling that I could if I would….

This rare combination of "the power on one side and the need on the other," as Roosevelt expressed it, came together first by extraordinary luck. He also knew that in politics, especially, luck does not last. So if he wished to share that luck with these men who helped him bring it about, he might only have a small window of opportunity.

This colonel loved his regiment. "My men" he often called them with a deeper more literal meaning than other commanders used the term. He corresponded regularly with many of the officers and attended each of the four reunions of the regiment held between 1899 and 1905. On his inauguration day in 1905, one of the most exciting days of his life, he scheduled a portion of the day for a visit exclusively with his Rough Riders honor guard and select cowboy friends. In 1911, when he came to Arizona to dedicate the dam named in his honor, he insisted on scheduling a luncheon for Rough Riders only. Not only his public writings and utterances, but also his private letters, give testimony to his devotion to "my men." A great many of the regiment proved themselves equally devoted to Roosevelt.

Four factors contributed to this unique and lasting relationship. First, there was the shared sense of urgency and purpose which the Spanish-American War generated. Second, Roosevelt's personality and preferred leadership style were personable and he made a strong effort to get to know the men in the regiment. The men of the Rough Riders were, after all, of the two types with which Roosevelt was most comfortable. The Ivy Leaguers who would volunteer to fight in a war were self-motivated and took direction well, and Roosevelt's experience with the more free-spirited cowboys seem to have given him a sense that these men would respond to collegial leadership better than they would to strict military authority. Third, Roosevelt was not a professional soldier and, therefore, did not feel the constraints of the military caste system. And finally, the men under Roosevelt's command were just few enough in number for the colonel to get to know the majority of them personally.

To keep alive the friendships forged in the war, the men of the regiment formed the "Roosevelt Rough Rider Association" during the last weeks at Camp Wikoff. Brodie was elected president while Roosevelt and Wood were designated vice presidents. Since Roosevelt had not yet gained notoriety in national politics, the name chosen by the organization would seem to indicate a deep connection between him and his men.

While governor of New York, Roosevelt expressed delight over the first two reunions which the association held in Las Vegas, New Mexico, and Oklahoma City respectively. These gatherings gave him a good excuse to travel west, and thereby keep his national reputation alive, without appearing to be neglecting his duties as governor. He reported after the first of these trips that "At every station…I was received by dense throngs exactly as if I had been a presidential candidate."

The first Rough Rider reunion was filled with ballyhoo and good humor. In addressing his old regiment, Roosevelt said that nothing could have taken him away from Albany at that time except this reunion. The statement was untrue, but the sentiment was probably genuine, and it was mutual.[22] Roosevelt was named the "permanent honorary president" of the association at that reunion. Specific political issues were not discussed.

Colorado lawman Sherman Bell, late of K troop, declared to his comrades that "the only politics of the Rough Riders is Roosevelt." This unique politics of Roosevelt was already, and would remain, devout, almost religious, and widespread among the Rough Riders and their associates. Lafayette Young, a Des Moines newspaper man who had been with the regiment as a reporter in Cuba, attended the reunion and made a speech which captured this spirit. He declared the "possibility of even-handed justice for all" as demonstrated by Colonel Roosevelt to be one of three "new gospels" advanced since the Civil War.

A spirit of affection between the Rough Riders and the small New Mexico town of Las Vegas prevailed throughout

---

22 According to one of Roosevelt's own letters, during the summer with the legislature out of session there was little for the governor to do.

—

the reunion. Roosevelt, himself, got somewhat carried away in this mood. At one point he said to the cheering crowd "if New Mexico wants to be a state you can count me in, and I will go to Washington to speak for you or do anything you wish." Though Colonel Brodie had commanded the Arizona squadron, reorganization in Cuba had put one troop from New Mexico under his command. The citizens of Las Vegas presented him with a sword. Of little note at the time, a group of Rough Riders, including Edward Collier of Arizona, robbed the town post office.

If President McKinley had been finishing his second term in 1900 instead of his first, Roosevelt might very well have been the Republican presidential nominee that year. Under the conditions which existed, however, his preference was to run for a second term as governor fully aware that the volatile nature of New York politics made his position in his words "utterly unstable." His friend, Henry Cabot Lodge, began as early as July 1899 to try to convince him to accept the 1900 Republican nomination for vice president. At first Roosevelt said that he was inclined to follow that advice if the nomination for governor should be denied of him. However, boss Tom Platt may have misled Roosevelt later. Platt repeatedly assured Roosevelt that he would support Roosevelt for another term as governor, or at the very least, would not oppose him. In the early months of 1900, as the Republican national convention drew closer, Roosevelt became more reticent about the prospects of being vice president and more anxious to secure renomination for governor.

In his hesitancy to seek the vice presidential nomination, Roosevelt pleaded with friends all over the country to vote against him, but delegations were already committed. At the convention Lafayette Young, the newspaper man who had spoken at the Rough Rider reunion a year earlier, nominated the colonel. All the New York delegates voted for Roosevelt except one, Roosevelt himself. The entire Arizona delegation was committed to Roosevelt. To avoid voting against the colonel's wishes, Alexander Brodie resigned from the delegation. He did, however, attend the convention as Roosevelt's guest. Despite his efforts to avoid the nomination, Roosevelt was selected on the first ballot.

Quickly resigning himself to what he perceived to be the will of the people, McKinley's new running mate was eager to campaign. The second Rough Rider reunion in Oklahoma City in early July provided the candidate with reason to tour the heartland only a week after his nomination. At that reunion, the Rough Riders chipped in to purchase a wooden leg for comrade Charles Buckholdt who had his lower leg shot off, and several Rough Riders nearly got arrested along with their famous colonel because the Oklahoma governor was unhappy with their unauthorized use of national guard horses and equipment for a parade. The politicking was done coming and going. Roosevelt campaigned at seven Kansas towns and one place in Oklahoma on his way out.[23] While returning east, he stumped in Illinois and Ohio.

Unlike the 1898 gubernatorial campaign, uniformed Rough Riders were not part of this effort. The tactic had been of little value even when the war was fresh in the minds of the voters. But the Colonel did at times use some of his famous regiment on the stump, and they still provided excitement, and occasionally, cause for concern. After the election he recalled how one Rough Rider in South Dakota joined the campaign train and "on the third day shot a Populist editor for saying mean things bout me." The man apparently had a different perspective on the operation of politics from the eastern norm.

---

23 Roosevelt had been extremely popular in Kansas after the war in 1898. State Republicans even then officially nominated him for president in 1900, two years in the future.

"I loaned him a hundred and fifty dollars to defend himself," Roosevelt explained.

And after the election he notified me, with a delicious unconsciousness of the implied commentary on Dakota justice, that he thought he was all right because they had elected a Republican district attorney! And so he used the hundred and fifty dollars to square a horse transaction. Heaven only knows whether this meant that he had stolen a horse or not.

With, or in spite of, such help, President McKinley was reelected in 1900 and Roosevelt became vice president.

The antics of the colonel's wild westerners sometimes concerned and disappointed the vice president. But he was not surprised, and he was quick to point out that the majority of the Rough Riders were doing well in civilian life. In one amusing letter he recounted the news of those in the territories who were not doing well:

As Edith says at times we feel as if we were the parents of a thousand very large very bad children. Many of them have strong homicidal proclivities and are always shooting someone or getting shot…Corporal Jackson has been killed in a shooting scrape…He was an excellent soldier and a valuable man in the regiment, but he was also a professional gambler, and after payday he was one of the few men into whose pocket the money of the rest tended to gravitate. In yesterday's mail came a letter from an ex-captain in the regiment who had been made District Attorney in New Mexico and who is prosecuting another member of the regiment for murder. The latter had himself written to me, his letter running: "Dear Colonel: I write to you because I am in trouble. I have shot a lady in the eye. But Colonel I did not mean to shoot that lady. It was all an accident, *for I was shooting at my wife.*".... In Arizona the last I heard of one of my men was that he was heading a posse which was following a band of train robbers which I regret to say also numbered in its ranks another ex-Rough Rider....

That Roosevelt's new position encouraged his office seeking friends should not be surprising. At the same time he contended that as vice president he had no more influence than he had as governor and possibly less. In July 1901, he wrote to William H. H. Llewellyn, New Mexico Attorney General and former Rough Rider Captain:

I have had great trouble through men of the regiment writing to me for positions. Sometimes they are unfit, and I turn them down; but there are plenty of them who are fit for the positions they seek but who cannot expect to get them because there are others with greater capacity or greater influence. The Oklahoma men have bothered me particularly, seeming to be unable to understand that I cannot possibly dictate the appointment of postmasters, etc. I have asked for so many favors for men of the regiment that I am positively ashamed to go to a single department in Washington, and above all, to the War Department. Yet each trooper not unnaturally when he writes to me thinks that his own is the only case, and that if I chose to, I can surely do anything he wants.

The number of civilian positions which Roosevelt, as governor and as vice president, arranged for western Rough Riders seems to have been few. Tom Rynning told in his memoirs of one Texas Rough Rider who enlisted as the train was pulling out of San Antonio. The man had been a horse thief and Rynning told Colonel Wood, suggesting that the man would want a pardon if he performed well. After the war, again according to Rynning's story, then Governor Roosevelt not only arranged a pardon but also employed the former outlaw as a page. Charles "Happy Jack" Hodgdon of Prescott landed a job as a brakeman on a New York railroad through Roosevelt. "Happy Jack" had come to New York to offer his services as a "bouncer out" for Governor Roosevelt, having read in the newspaper that the Colonel was deluged by office seekers. Another Arizonan, George McCarter got on with the government printing office in Washington, DC. As vice president, Roosevelt secured the appointment of Arizonans David Warford as a forest ranger and Norman Orme as receiver of customs for the Dominican Republic. Orme, who had been severely wounded in Cuba, continued to work for the Treasury Department, was transferred to Washington, and became a regular visitor at the White House during Roosevelt's presidency.[24] Warford did not stay long as a forest ranger. Emilio Cassi, who had been the trumpeter during the gubernatorial campaign was turned down for a position. Roosevelt wrote him:

> ...it would help me immensely if you could have some private employment before appealing for a government position, because they are certain to ask as to where you were last employed and what you did there. Personally I have great confidence in you, but of course there would have to be much explanation in connection with that man you shot.[25]

---

24 Orme had been shot through the lung and his condition was so severe that doctors on the transport ship back to America ignored him, preferring to work on men who had a reasonable chance for survival. James McClintock reported in one of his 1931 radio broadcasts that Orme was back in the hospital because of the wound.

25 Cassi had returned to the service and was stationed again in Cuba. As a military policeman there he killed a Cuban official. The killing may or may not have been justified, but the political situation in Cuba made his acquittal unlikely. While imprisoned in Cuba, he married a wealthy Cuban woman who obtained his freedom by divulging a plot by rebels to blow up two government buildings.

Roosevelt was more enthusiastic about his aide, Henry Bardshar, who wanted to be a consul in some Spanish speaking country. Bardshar had secured recommendations from the Arizona governor and the city attorney of Prescott. To these Roosevelt added his observation of Bardshar's "absolute fearlessness and loyal devotion" and his personal belief in Bardshar's integrity while confessing that "I have had no opportunity to test him in civilian life." No position materialized for the young man at that time.

The third Rough Rider reunion in Colorado Springs caused the vice president, some anxiety. When the date selected conflicted with Roosevelt's schedule, the date and location of the reunion were changed to coincide with Colorado's quarter-centennial celebration at which the vice president was scheduled to speak. This was an accommodation which he viewed as an embarrassment. And while a few of the prominent Rough Riders did hail from the Colorado Springs area, Colorado had not been among the major staging areas for recruitment.[26] Naturally Vice President Roosevelt was concerned that by being too conspicuous under these circumstances the Rough Riders might discredit themselves or him. He suggested that other western volunteer organizations be invited and that veterans festivities center around Colorado veterans including those of the Civil War. Roosevelt feared that the continuation of annual reunions would be detrimental to the reputation of the regiment, and he sought the help of other former officers in ending them. His efforts were successful. No more regimental reunions were held until 1905.

---

26 Professional lawmen Benjamin Daniels and Sherman Bell had both come to San Antonio from eastern Colorado. Both were very highly regarded by Roosevelt. Bell became the adjutant general of the Colorado National Guard and served in that position for many years. Incidentally, Edward Collier, the Rough Rider who had robbed the post office in Las Vegas, New Mexico, was in prison in Colorado on an unrelated charge at the time. Some of the Rough Rider officers at the reunion made an appeal for a pardon for him.

But a certain cohesiveness had been established. These men expected to continue their association, and many remained lifelong friends. Roosevelt remained their unquestionable leader, and a truly uncommon, paternalistic loyalty was growing between the Colonel and his men. He would always have the power and they the need, but he would never forget that his power was earned because they followed him up a hill in Cuba. The best years for the Colonel's men were soon to come, especially in Arizona where a flood of appointments began in 1902 after Alexander Brodie was appointed governor.

CHAPTER 4

A Little Water and a Few Good Citizens

A story is told of William Tecumseh Sherman after the Civil War when he was assigned to command the army of the west. The famous general was known to have an unfavorable opinion of Arizona. One Arizonan defended the territory in a discussion with Sherman saying, "Ah, Arizona isn't so bad; all it needs is a little water and a little less heat" to which the general replied "Huh! That's all hell needs."[27]

Besides less heat and more water, we might speculate that both hell and the Arizona Territory of 1901 could have benefited from a few good citizens well placed in leadership roles. Eventually Colonel Roosevelt would provide water and a few good civil leaders. But for the present he was trying to adjust to the position of vice president. He could see some advantages to the job at first, but he was realistic about his own temperament. Shortly after assuming the office, he wrote to a friend:

---

27   Bert M. Fireman, *Arizona: Historic Land,* (New York: Alfred A. Knopf, 1982): 3.

I have really enjoyed presiding over the Senate for the week the extra session lasted. I shall get fearfully tired in the future no doubt and of course I should like a more active position. But it is an office of <great> honor and dignity; and when I think of the great variety of opinions which I have expressed with extreme freedom and with not an altogether judicious absence of reserve on every conceivable subject, the wonder is that I should ever have been elected to it.

A month later he was still philosophical about the position, but hardly happy, saying, "…I greatly miss in the Vice-Presidency the active work of all the positions I have previously held, yet I really *feel* that I have been so fortunate and have been so amply rewarded that I have not only no cause for complaint but even cause for profound gratitude." Not long after this he became more pessimistic about his job, calling it "an utterly anomalous office (one which ought to be abolished)…."

"The man who occupies it," he continued, "may at any moment be everything; but meanwhile he is practically nothing."

In September 1901 William McKinley was assassinated and Roosevelt went from "practically nothing" to president of the United States. "It is a dreadful thing to come into the Presidency this way," he said, "but it would be far worse to be morbid about it." Though keeping McKinley's cabinet, Roosevelt soon began to make the presidency his.

United States presidents then had a special relationship with the territories aspiring to become states, appointing most important executive officers. When Roosevelt came to the office, he was of course already intimately connected with the four territories of the contiguous United States. His meteoric rise in politics had begun, after all, as a leader of men from these territories. This new president knew personally and intimately hundreds of men in these territories, many of whom were leading citizens. By placing his favorite and most loyal friends in high positions, Roosevelt might exert strong presidential influence on these territories. And of course for the common soldiers among the Rough Riders, the "power" component of that "unique combination of power and need" which allows a man to help another had expanded many times over now that the colonel occupied the White House. Many, perhaps most, quickly saw the opportunities before them.

Roosevelt empathized with the westerners like no previous president since Andrew Jackson. And the thought of being the president to bring the last territories into the union, thus completing the contiguous United States after having led men from the territories into glorious victory in war, must have also been appealing to Roosevelt, the historian. On December 3, 1901, in his first speech to Congress, the new president took up the cause which had been advocated by the National Irrigation Congress. Using the same arguments which Buckey O'Neill had used at the 1896 Irrigation Congress in Phoenix and which had since been adopted as standard NIC rhetoric, he said:

> It is right for the national government to make the streams and rivers of the arid region useful by engineering works of storage as to make useful the rivers and harbors of the humid region by engineering works of another kind. The storage of the floods in the reservoirs at the headwaters of our rivers is but an enlargement of our present policy of river control, under which levees are built on the lower reaches of these same streams.

The Newlands Reclamation Bill had been narrowly defeated on March 1, 1901. President McKinley had endorsed the bill but did not exert his influence for its passage. Even westerners were divided about the proposal at that time, but their division was not great. The annual irrigation congresses had been held for over a decade. Westerners at these conferences generally agreed that reclamation of the arid regions would require some type of federal government loans or subsidies. Disagreement existed chiefly over the relative amount of federal control verses local autonomy.

In 1899, the National Irrigation Congress met in the east for the first time and attitudes of easterners surprised the delegates. Eastern opposition to nationally sponsored western irrigation projects did not appear to be widespread. Now, with the full support of the President, the time had finally come for action. The National Reclamation Act, supported by Roosevelt, passed, and was signed into law on July 17, 1902. Buckey O'Neill would have been pleased.

While the reclamation bill was making its way through Congress, President Roosevelt created excitement in Arizona in a very different way. He had been in the White House barely a month when a Rough Rider in Arizona sent him a letter requesting an appointment as US marshal for the territory. The writer had read a newspaper account of a possible scandal, and speculation about the removal of the incumbent, Myron McCord. As it turned out, no charges were forthcoming, but the applicant, Benjamin F. Daniels, had so endeared himself to Roosevelt by his service in Cuba that the President decided to replace Marshal McCord with this new man immediately. McCord had only held the marshalcy for about seven months when he was notified of his dismissal, and he was a formidable man to be turned out so quickly and without cause. He had been Arizona's territorial governor at the outbreak of the Spanish-American War but resigned to lead a regiment of Arizona volunteers which had been formed after the Rough Riders. (They did not get to Cuba.) He also owned the *Phoenix Gazette,* and he was a former president of the Arizona Associated Press.

McCord's proposed replacement, Ben Daniels, had an impressive background in law enforcement. He had been an assistant city marshal of Dodge City, Kansas under the famous Bill Tilghman. Former Dodge City mayor Robert Wright would later write of Tilghman and Daniels, "No braver men ever handled a gun or arrested an outlaw, and Dodge City never passed through a tougher time." Daniels also served as marshal of Guthrie, Oklahoma, agent for Wells Fargo Company, and night marshal of Cripple Creek, Colorado. From Cripple Creek he traveled with fellow lawman Sherman Bell to San Antonio where they joined Roosevelt's regiment.

The Senate held up confirmation of Marshal Daniels, because at the time of the appointment a gambling establishment in Nogales employed him as a card dealer. Some few but persistent citizens objected to having a professional gambler as their marshal. The arguments were conspicuous front-page news in the *Arizona Republic*, the territory's leading newspaper. The story also received an inordinate amount of coverage in other Arizona newspaper, enough to suggest that Myron McCord may have been exercising his influence with his journalist colleagues to block Daniels' nomination. Republican newspapers were, however, rightfully upset that the popular Republican, McCord, was thrown out in favor of Daniels, a Democrat. The *Tucson Daily Citizen* joked, "Well, at least the President had to go outside the Republican Party to find a Square Dealer."

Daniels' nomination was confirmed on January 22, 1902, but during the controversy the Senate had expanded the investigation of his background. The day after the confirmation Senator Henry Moore Teller of Colorado proposed that the Senate review the appointment in light of new evidence. A letter which he had just received from a Kansas man suggested that Ben Daniels may have committed at least two murders. One of the killings occurred during the "county seat war" in which Daniels and his associates absconded with the county records. One man was killed, but Daniels was never tried for this killing though four of his associates were. They were found not guilty.

The other killing was more deliberate and the facts more damning. On April 16, 1886, on a Dodge City street, Ben Daniels shot Ed Julien in the back. After Julien fell, Daniels fired three more rounds into Julien's body. Daniels was arrested and tried for murder but escaped conviction by an even six-six vote. Letters received by the President and passed to the Senate claimed that Julien had owned a restaurant in Dodge while Daniels operated a saloon next door. The letters contended that the noise from Daniels' saloon bothered customers in Julien's restaurant, and Julien obtained a court order to close the saloon. This angered Daniels which led to the shooting.

Mayor Wright told a different story in his written testimony for the Senate. He said that Julien was a cowboy whom Daniels had arrested for disturbing the peace. Sometime later Julien made threats around town concerning Daniels. Wright further claimed that Daniels came to him with this information seeking advice and Julien was killed minutes after that meeting.

The facts of the case, as reported in local newspapers at the time of the killing, suggest that Wright attempted to put a positive spin on the killing. Julien had been arrested seventeen months earlier for disturbing the peace, the result of a fight in his restaurant.[28] While this incident may have been the beginning of bad blood between Julien and Daniels, it was not a major factor in the killing a year and a half later. In the Dodge City election of 1886, Julien actively supported the reform faction which pledged to enforce the Kansas prohibition law. Daniels

---

28   "Police Court Doings," *Dodge City Democrat*, November 15, 1884. In Nyle H. Miller and Joseph W. Snell, *Great Gunfighters of the Kansas Cowtowns*, (Lincoln: University of Nebraska Press, 1973): 428.

had only recently become involved in running the saloon. When the reformers won the election, Daniels was forced to resign as deputy city marshal. On the day of the shooting, Daniels had been served with a court order closing his saloon. During the trial the defense claimed that Julian appeared to have been reaching in his coat for a gun when Daniels shot him. A gun was found on Julien's body, but witnesses expressed doubt that Julien ever had the chance to go for his gun.

The Senate had not yet completed the investigation of the Julien killing when word came from Wyoming that Benjamin Daniels had been convicted and served three years in prison there for the theft of government mules. Roosevelt, who had backed Daniels completely throughout the investigation and had secured Daniels' word that he hid nothing, inquired whether there might be more than one Ben Daniels. But prison identification records clearly indicated that this Ben Daniels had been an inmate of the United States Penitentiary at Laramie City, Wyoming.[29] When the truth could finally be denied no longer, Daniels admitted his prison record and resigned as marshal. His explanation to Roosevelt was that he had simply forgot about the three years of his life spent in federal prison. The Senate investigation ended without a full report on the Julian killing and with at least two other minor accusations against the now ex-marshal pending.[30]

The marshal affair had frustrated and embarrassed the President. On February 22, he wrote to Daniels, "You put me in the attitude of unwittingly deceiving the Senate and of

---

29 Daniels was described as pock marked and missing the right ear lobe. When asked about the ear, Daniels would always say it was bitten off in a fight. He told Roosevelt that this fight occurred when he went to arrest a man. This is probably untrue because Daniels was quite young when he entered the penitentiary and the ear lobe was already missing then. It is possible that the lobe was cut off to brand Daniels as a horse thief as this was the custom at the time.

30 Daniels was also accused of stealing $600 from a gambling establishment in La Junta, Colorado and extorting money from businesses while acting as night marshal of Cripple Creek, Colorado. In fairness though, it should be noted that one letter in his appointment file praises him for fine police work in Cripple Creek.

establishing a precedent which was bound to return and plague me. So I must ask you to send me your resignation." Amazingly though in the same letter he also wrote:

> I am sure that you are telling the truth, and that you would be a first-class Marshal. I like you and trust you, and would employ you without hesitation in my private business....

> Now Sheriff, I want to say a word most earnestly to you. This is a hard blow to you, and you can best show the stuff that is in you by the way you bear it. If you weaken and do anything of which you and your friends have cause to be ashamed, you will justify all that your enemies say about you, and you will wreck yourself forever. If you stand straight and go about your duties as a man, you will do for yourself what no one else can do for you—you will give the lie to your enemies and you will put yourself in a position where in the future men who believe in you, as I believe in you, will be able to repose trust in you, and use you in a responsible position.

These words proved to be quite sincere. In the meantime, Myron McCord was recommissioned and allowed to serve as marshal until the end of his term in 1905. Roosevelt was to take a very remarkable interest in promoting the welfare and career of Ben Daniels. Less than a month after the marshal fiasco, the President wrote to Mrs. Daniels that "If Ben would like a deputyship under Marshal McCord, I think I can see that he gets it."

Even without the help of Roosevelt, Rough Riders in Arizona gravitated into the law enforcement profession though most had no prior experience in law enforcement. Charles Utting, a Phoenix cowboy who had served in B Troop, became a deputy US marshal under McCord. Three other B Troop veterans were hired by Burton Mossman, first captain of the Arizona Rangers, for his small force of thirteen. As originally chartered by the Arizona legislature, the Rangers were to consist of a captain, one sergeant, and twelve privates. For the elite position of sergeant, Mossman chose Rough Rider John Foster, who had been a miner at the time of his enlistment in Roosevelt's cavalry. Rough Riders John E. Campbell and Richard Stanton were enlisted as privates. Campbell had been a soldier before his Rough Rider days and had also later enlisted to fight in the Philippine insurrection. Stanton apparently had law enforcement experience because he listed his occupation as "policeman" at the time of his recruitment into the Rough Riders.

Ranger Stanton proved to be a disappointment. He apparently had some trouble with authority or with getting along with people. He had irritated his Rough Rider commander, James McClintock, by his abrasiveness and complaining in San Antonio. Lieutenant Richard Day also had trouble with Trooper Stanton's insubordination during combat.[31] Shortly after enlisting in the Rangers, Stanton supposedly picked a fight with a fellow Ranger. In the course of the scuffle Ranger Bert Grover, who interceded, was wounded slightly in the right leg when his gun went off accidentally. Stanton was subsequently discharged from the Rangers "for the good of the service." However, in fairness to Stanton it should be noted that Grover was known to be a bit of a brawler himself.

The Rangers along with the rest of Arizona saw some major changes beginning in June 1902. At that time, President Roosevelt appointed the Rough Riders' old Arizona squadron commander, Alexander Brodie, as governor. George Smalley, Governor Brodie's secretary and speech writer, claimed that

---

31 David Hughes, "A Story of the 'Rough Riders." Unpublished manuscript, David Hughes Papers, Arizona Pioneer Historical Society, Tucson.

Brodie had gone to Washington along with Colonel William Christie to secure the governorship for Christie, but the President instead insisted that Brodie take the position. This story has been often repeated, but in actuality Roosevelt wanted Brodie for governor all along and Brodie knew it, though he still hoped for a good opportunity to get back into the army. In May 1901, then Vice President Roosevelt wrote to Brodie, "I do wish you could be made governor." On October 19, 1901, less than a month after Roosevelt assumed the presidency, Brodie wrote to his friend James McClintock that he had just returned from Washington where he had a long talk with the President regarding Arizona in which nothing was decided yet. But Arizona newspapers were already reporting that Brodie had been selected as governor. By mid-December Roosevelt's choice was definite but still unannounced. The incumbent Arizona governor had not yet resigned.

Governor Nathan O. Murphy was popular and had in fact been the Republican nominee for congressional delegate in 1900, and he was in the middle of his term. His position became shaky when questions arose about his use of territorial funds. The governor then further alienated the President and many Arizonans by going to Washington in January 1902 to lobby against the reclamation bill. As mentioned earlier, the federal reclamation program was controversial because of the issue of federal control. Murphy opposed federal control of western irrigation. He was correct in his interpretation that, as it was written, the reclamation bill could only create new communities, not improve existing ones such as Phoenix. But with the expectation that flaws would be corrected later, the majority of Arizonans favored the bill. The Tucson *Citizen* criticized the governor for lobbying on behalf of "private monopolies at the expense of the public interest." At about the same time, the personal conduct of Governor Murphy came under criticism in the form of "innumerable letters" to the

President.[32] Soon after his Washington trip Governor Murphy resigned. His replacement, Alexander Brodie, was much more philosophically in tune with the President, and Roosevelt could put complete trust in him. Brodie would defer to Roosevelt on most issues. The one important exception was the question of Arizona statehood.

Arizona's new governor took office on July 1, 1902. In his inaugural address he called Roosevelt "the greatest of Americans." Brodie's administration is known to have been successful and remarkably free of scandal. Part of the credit might be given to sage advice from the former governor of New York. Roosevelt wrote to Brodie in June 1902:

> Be exceedingly careful in anything you do about the funds of the Territory. From a long experience in politics I cannot too strongly say that the worst of all mistakes is to have any kind of trouble concerning public moneys. Take no chances and pay no heed to any personal or political friend's advice in the matter of the bestowing of public funds, any more than in the matter of the letting of contracts.

Brodie strictly heeded the advice, even refusing small supplemental funds allocated specifically for him by the legislature. He probably also remembered the problems of his predecessor.

The last sentence of the letter quoted above is interesting. Here Roosevelt said, "When you take office and appoint Ben Daniels, let me know, as I want to write to him." The two had agreed that Brodie would appoint Daniels as superintendent of the territorial prison at Yuma. The President confided the deal to his secretary of state, John Hay, and Hay replied that the proverb should be "Set a Rough Rider to catch a thief." The plan was changed when the new governor with the consultation

---

32 Jay J. Wagoner, *Arizona Territory 1848-1912*: 364

and consent of the President bowed to pressure to appoint a different candidate to the superintendency. In August Brodie asked Daniels, "as a favor" to both himself and the President, to take the position of assistant superintendent of the prison "until something to which he (Daniels) is specially fitted turns up."[33] Daniels turned down the offer.[34]

The Yuma Prison became a source of jobs for many Rough Riders. Walter Gregory, who was the son of a former Tucson mayor and had been near death from fever in Cuba, was named secretary and storekeeper. According to the Yuma *Sentinel* five Rough Riders became guards at the prison shortly after Brodie took office.[35] Guard Sebird Henderson was unhappy with his job and, being an expert rider, soon joined Buffalo Bill's show when it came to Phoenix. Howard Marine, on the other hand, served with some distinction and is credited with helping to foil an attempted prison break in which the prison superintendent and his assistant were held hostage. Rough Rider sergeant Charles E. McGarr also started a career in law enforcement by first serving as a prison guard for two years. He went on to serve as a deputy US marshal and an Arizona Ranger.

As president, Roosevelt rarely denied an appointment to a qualified Rough Rider, and he actively sought to place the key officers of the regiment in important positions in the territories. The realities of national politics, however, did occasionally prevent such an appointment. James McClintock applied for the job as Arizona's Territorial Secretary. He was shocked and disappointed when the position he sought was denied. His leg was permanently disabled, and he had been

---

33 This is revealed in a letter from Roosevelt to Brodie dated July 22, 1902.

34 Two other Rough Riders were eager for the assistant prison superintendent job which Daniels declined. They were Wesley A. Hill and Richard Stanton, the latter having recently been discharged from the Arizona Rangers "for the good of the service."

35 Among the new prison guards appointed in 1902 was Richard Stanton who had been dismissed from the Arizona Rangers for quarreling. He apparently found a niche as a prison guard. By 1909, he was still with the prison.

granted only a small disability pension with which he was displeased. The position went to Isaac Stoddard, who had hoped to be governor and had the backing of influential New York Republicans, including the President's close friend Henry Cabot Lodge.

Governor Brodie encouraged McClintock to apply for the job of Phoenix postmaster and endorsed the captain's candidacy. Roosevelt made the appointment in the summer of 1902. McClintock seems to have regarded the duties of postmaster lightly because in applying for the job he stated that he wanted it so that he would have time to pursue his writing. He probably did not have a great deal of time for writing though. He was organizing the Arizona branch of the Spanish War Veterans Association, and his friend, the governor also appointed him as a colonel commanding the first regiment of infantry of the Arizona National Guard.

The new governor's most important appointment that first summer was the captaincy of the Arizona Rangers. Captain Burton Mossman had been compelled to resign following a disturbance in Bisbee in which he was involved.[36] Brodie selected fellow Rough Rider Tom Harbo Rynning to replace Mossman. Rynning claimed in his memoirs that he never sought the job but Brodie and Roosevelt both insisted he take it. The Rangers had established a generally good record under Mossman, but they are remembered best as Rynning's crew. Mossman had commanded the Rangers for only a year while Rynning was on the job for four and a half years. Rynning had spent several years in the army as a young man. As a civilian he had, until now, made his living as a building contractor.

---

36 Mossman and two of his Rangers had become involved in a brawl with local law enforcement officials in Bisbee. This was the result of a dispute over a poker game. The affair led to a petition to have Mossman removed. This may have been partially politically motivated because local lawmen were known to be jealous and uncooperative regarding the Rangers. Mossman next became a deputy marshal under Myron McCord.

Captain Rynning remade the force in his own image beginning by moving the Rangers from Bisbee to Douglas where he thought more criminal activity occurred. Intensive training in marksmanship and police tactics became standard for all new recruits despite the fact that many were already skilled with firearms. A large turnover of personnel occurred among the Rangers when the new captain took charge thus allowing Rynning to select his own personnel. He does not, however, appear to have intentionally caused the turnover. It was more likely due to natural attrition. Ranger pay was low, and high turnover was common throughout the history of the force. Coincidental with the change at the top in 1902, the one-year enlistments of Mossman's Rangers were expiring. On assuming command Rynning stated publicly that he hoped to retain Mossman's men. But within eight months under Rynning, only three of Mossman's force remained on the roll despite the fact that the strength of the Rangers had been nearly doubled by then (from fourteen to twenty-six).

Contrary to popular belief, Captain Rynning did not show a strong preference for the men of the old regiment in hiring Arizona Rangers. True, John E. Campbell, the only Rough Rider among the Mossman holdovers, was promoted while the other two were not. He took one of the four sergeant positions which opened in the new organizational structure of the expanded force. However, Campbell simply appears to have been a valuable man. He was slightly older than most of the other Rough Riders and had a long and impressive military record. He had served in the regular army before enlisting in the Rough Riders. As a first sergeant at the San Juan battle, he won Roosevelt's praise in the colonel's official report. He was highly esteemed by Captain McClintock who called him "a soldier of rare ability, whom lack of education alone kept in the ranks of a non-commissioned officer." He enlisted again to serve in the Philippines where he again won first sergeant stripes. After returning to Arizona, he joined the National Guard and was commissioned a second lieutenant. Rough Rider John Foster had been second in command as the only Ranger sergeant under Cap Mossman but resigned to become a deputy marshal. He rejoined the Rangers when Rynning took over and became his second in command with the rank of lieutenant.

Only four more Rough Riders would be hired by Rynning for the Rangers during his entire tenure and none of these was promoted beyond private. They are Charles McGarr, Oscar J. Mullen, fast gun and hot tempered William W. Webb, and David Warford who had apparently already tired of his life as a forest ranger. Mullen had earlier aspired to be postmaster of Tempe. Unable to secure that position, he asked the help of his C Troop captain, J. L. B. Alexander to get "anything for which I am fitted, providing there is some money in it," but he balked at Alexander's suggestion that he could be a guard at the Yuma prison. He served only three months with the Rangers. Warford lasted little more and was discharged for drunkenness. Campbell's health may have been failing; he served only four months under Rynning. Webb and McGarr both served a one-year enlistment then resigned. McGarr became a deputy US marshal.

John Foster was the only Rough Rider to serve more than one year under Captain Rynning.[37] Of 105 men who served in the Rangers under three different captains, only seven were Rough Riders. Mossman hired three of those seven for his fourteen-man force in his one year as captain. Rynning, commanding a force of twenty-six for over four years, hired only four more Rough Riders. The last captain did not hire any Rough Riders. Only two Rough Riders served for more than one year as Rangers and they were both hired originally

---

37 Rynning had great respect for Foster as an officer, calling him "the best combination of coolness and brains among the men who worked in the field.

by Mossman. The Rough Riders certainly did not dominate the Ranger force at any time. What influence the Rough Riders did have on the Rangers was through Captain Rynning, Governor Brodie, and, beginning in 1906, US Attorney J. L. B. Alexander.

The original purpose of the Rangers, to stop cattle rustling, was done so effectively by Captain Mossman's charges during the first year that the Rangers were freed to deal with additional tasks. Under Rynning's command and Brodie's direction the Rangers came to be employed more as a territorial police force, keeping the peace during miners' strikes and attempting to root out Mexican revolutionaries operating out of southern Arizona, thereby threatening the neutrality of the United States in Mexico's internal problems. They also continued to be controversial and disliked by some local officials.

One of the most controversial incidents involving Rynning's Rangers was the shooting of a saloon proprietor in Douglas by Ranger (and former Rough Rider) William W. Webb. The victim, Lorenzo "Lon" Bass[38] had had a confrontation with Webb and later threatened to kill the Ranger if he entered the saloon again. According to the Rangers, on the night of February 8, 1903, Webb entered the saloon with another Ranger to investigate shots heard fired in the vicinity. Bass accosted Webb, and Webb drew quickly and shot him twice, once through the heart. Webb was arrested but exonerated. On the day of the hearing though, a fire destroyed the saloon and with it any physical evidence which may have existed. Fires were a common problem in the frontier towns then, and this one was traced to a conflict between a prostitute and her client. The only suspicious event involved with the fire was that firefighters had an unusually difficult time getting water pressure for the fire hose. The Rangers were not suspected

---

38 Lorenzo had a famous brother, Sam Bass.

or implicated. Webb remained on the force until the end of his one-year enlistment.

That Arizona even needed rangers at all was looked upon by some as an indication that this was still the untamed frontier. Leaders of the territory were actively trying to alter this image in 1902 because Arizona statehood was under serious consideration by the US Congress. On May 9, a bill to provide for the admission of Arizona, New Mexico, and Oklahoma was passed by the House of Representatives. But the Senate Committee on Territories was cool to statehood for Arizona and New Mexico. They voted to postpone action on the bill until the next session of Congress.

Committee chairman Senator Albert Beveridge arranged a fact-finding mission to go to the territories in November. The committee's schedule was deliberately indefinite, and they announced that they did not want to be entertained formally. They showed up in Prescott, a town which was not on their itinerary, a day before they were due in Arizona. In Phoenix, the committee was met by Governor Brodie, former governor Murphy, Representative Smith, and other dignitaries. Brodie lectured them about the quality of Arizona schools which he called "second to none." He pointed out that Arizona possessed the largest belt of pine timber in the United States. And he showed the committee a model of a proposed dam on the Salt River at the site selected by McClintock and his colleagues back in 1889 which he (Brodie) hoped would be the first project under the Newlands Reclamation Act.[39] The next day Governor Brodie accompanied the committee to Tucson and Bisbee. Despite the efforts of territorial officials to accommodate and impress their important Washington guests, the committee reported its opposition to statehood for both

---

39 Governor Brodie had included a plea for the Salt River dam project in his first annual report to the Secretary of the Interior. (Larry Waite Kittell, "The Administration of Alexander O. Brodie, Arizona Territorial Governor, 1902-1905," University of Arizona, Master's thesis, 1973.)

New Mexico and Arizona along with the recommendation that the Indian Territory be joined to Oklahoma.

The most compelling argument for rejection of Arizona and New Mexico was insufficient population. Arizona contained only 123,000 non-Indians while New Mexico had 195,000. Beveridge believed, not unreasonably, that such sparsely populated western states were coming to dominate the Senate and thereby forcing the will of a relatively small minority upon the great decisions of the nation.[40]

He finally came to support a compromise by which Arizona and New Mexico would be joined into one large state. The senator, a nationalist, expansionist, and progressive, was a strong and important ally of President Roosevelt. The President endorsed the plan, deferring to the senator's leadership in this matter concerning his domain, but Governor Brodie became an outspoken opponent. Roosevelt tolerated Brodie's opposition on this one issue, perhaps because he did not wholeheartedly support the plan himself and he knew that Governor Brodie was speaking for the vast majority of Arizonans. To remove Brodie would only have excited the already strong and united opposition in the territory, even if Roosevelt had been so inclined. He was not; and the Rough Riders Brodie and Roosevelt may not have been as far apart in their visions of Arizona as was then perceived.

Roosevelt's letters indicate that he probably agreed more with Beveridge's contention that the population of Arizona was too small to warrant statehood than he did with the jointure proposal. The difference between Roosevelt and Beveridge seems to be that Roosevelt saw that with irrigation Arizona had the potential to attract a sufficient population. For the President, the thing to do was to delay and discourage the appeal for statehood. The energies and resources of the pro-

---

40   John Braeman, Albert J. Beveridge: *American Nationalist*

—

statehood element in Arizona could be diverted to the fight against jointure. How strongly Governor Brodie really favored statehood in 1902 is not known. Having run for Congress in 1898 on a platform centered on immediate statehood for Arizona the governor was not free to profess a change of heart, but by 1903 he privately believed that Arizona should remain a territory for the time being.[41]

The issue of statehood and the associated threat of jointure were concerns of Governor Brodie, but he had little hope of controlling these issues. The Twenty-second Legislature, which opened in January 1903, was a more practical concern. Brodie's opening address was well received and did bring about one important change. His top priority was to have corporate filing fees, which, at that time, were paid directly to the territorial secretary, placed in the territorial treasury. Arizona had liberal incorporation laws at that time, and the secretary was able to make an estimated $40,000 to $50,000 beyond his regular salary from collecting the fees making him by far the best paid official in the territory.[42] This was clearly an oversight which needed to be corrected. Secretary Isaac Stoddard was unapologetic about the appearance of graft and he opposed this infringement on his position. A personal and political rivalry resulted between Stoddard and Brodie. The legislation proposed by the governor, however, was passed into law and applauded throughout the territory.

The governor had no real impact on any other significant legislation during that session. He was unsuccessful in getting the legislature to tax the mines for a more reasonable share of the tax burden. Previous governors had also proposed increasing the taxes paid by the mines which were thought to be ridiculously low. In other areas, Governor Brodie proposed

---

41 This is reveled in a letter written by Governor Brodie's personal secretary to his father. George Smalley Papers, Arizona Pioneers Historical Society, Tucson.

42 Jay J. Wagoner, *Arizona Territory 1863–1912:* 404.

a contribution by the territory for the support of the Arizona Pioneers' Historical Society, of which he was a long-time member, and the legislature granted $1000. The Governor signed the bill which established the eight-hour workday for underground miners though he stated some misgivings about it.[43] And, he vetoed women's suffrage, explaining that he felt that the veto was necessary because the Organic Act of 1863 which created the Arizona Territory permitted only males to vote. The Arizona Territory did not, therefore, in his opinion, have the authority to grant women the right to vote. Despite the outward appearance, Governor Brodie was not the only obstacle to women's suffrage in Arizona. The suffrage bill had passed the Arizona House as a joke. It was then endorsed by the Council only because the Governor had promised to veto it.[44]

While the Twenty-second Legislature was in session, the hated joint statehood proposal was under discussion in the US Congress. Surprisingly, the Council, Arizona's upper house, voted to endorse the plan. The next day, however, the Arizona House of Representatives voted unanimously to oppose jointure. Given that information, Delegate Marcus Smith in Washington declared that Arizona would always oppose joint statehood.

The joint statehood issue did not, however, anger Arizonans so much that they did not want to see and cheer their president. In May 1903, Roosevelt went on a speech making tour of the west with a stop at the Grand Canyon. The President was joined by Governor Brodie and several other Rough Riders, "most of them," he admitted frankly in a private letter, "with homicidal pasts." Ben Daniels was, of course, among the group. He told one reporter that he wanted to show the President that he was not afraid to meet with

---

43 Brodie had some reason for misgivings. The eight-hour law was in the best interest of justice and humanity for miners, but it did lead to labor conflicts.
44 Jay J. Wagoner, 406.

him. Roosevelt's response on seeing Daniels was described in the *Arizona Republican* as "cordial in the extreme" to which "Daniels was almost overcome."

At the Canyon rim near Bright Angel Lodge, the President spoke to the crowd of about one thousand. He naturally began by talking about his regiment and those officers from Arizona who had most impressed him.

> …as long as I live it will be to me an inspiration to have served with Buckey O'Neill. I have met so many comrades whom I prize, for whom I feel only respect and admiration, and I shall not particularize among them except to say that there is no one for whom I feel more of respect and admiration and affection than for your governor.

Roosevelt later made reference to the project which was to be his greatest achievement in Arizona: "Arizona is one of the regions from which I expect most development through the wise action of the national congress in passing the irrigation act. The first and biggest experiment now in view under that act is the one that we are trying in Arizona." The President was, of course, referring to the Salt River dam project, the dream for which Brodie, O'Neill, and McClintock had all contributed so much and in so doing insured that Arizona's star would rise.

From the Grand Canyon, the President went on to California, Oregon, and Washington then returned to the east through the nation's heartland, stopping to make speeches all along the route. He arrived back in the capital June 5.

Governor Brodie also journeyed east at the time, leaving Secretary Stoddard as acting governor when a strike broke out in the copper mining town of Morenci. The new eight-hour workday legislation for underground miners, which was designed to protect the miners' health, precipitated the strike. The miners resisted the reduction in wages which accompanied the reduction in hours. The operators offered a compromise. They proposed nine hours pay for eight hours work, but the pay scale at Morenci was already lower than in the rest of the territory. The company claimed that the lower grade ore in the area necessitated lower pay, but the miners believed that the real reason was racism. Eighty to ninety percent of the miners were Mexican or Mexican American. In racially mixed communities of Arizona, Hispanics were only allowed to work in the low paying jobs on the surface, not underground.

Stoddard viewed the strike as potentially very dangerous. He moved to end it quickly, first by ordering the Arizona Rangers to go immediately to Morenci to prevent violence. The twenty-four Rangers who responded under Captain Rynning joined a like number of local officials. While this small number acquitted themselves bravely, they were in a very difficult position, greatly outnumbered by well-armed strikers. The entire Arizona National Guard was rushed to the scene, two hundred thirty men under the command of Colonel James McClintock. Stoddard wired for federal assistance also, and Roosevelt quickly dispatched troops.

That no bloodshed occurred from the strike can be largely attributed to a sudden violent rainstorm and devastating flood which struck when tensions were high and only the Rangers and sheriff's deputies were on the scene confronted by angry strikers. Rynning and his Rangers deserve credit for defusing the situation as best they could by arresting key leaders of the strike while avoiding much direct confrontation. Roosevelt and McClintock could be congratulated up to this point too. The restraint shown by the strikers seems to have gone unnoticed and unappreciated because a few were attempting to rally the majority to violence. This, however, is all the more reason to praise the overall non-violent nature of the strike.

While the President could claim that violence was avoided through the quick response of the government, this affair does not reflect well on the President or Arizona. Already the day after the federal troops had arrived, the *Arizona Republican* was reporting that the strike was over and the mines would soon reopen. No follow-up investigation was ordered by Roosevelt, Stoddard, or Brodie. A matter-of-fact report in the *Republican* appears to indicate that the government was used by the company to break up the strike:

Many Mexicans have been trying to sell their houses here preparatory to leaving the district. It is believed that the Italians will not be allowed to return to work. Events of the near future will decide if the Clifton-Moreci district shall be made a white man's camp.

The power of the territorial and federal governments appeared, at least, to have been manipulated by management to break the strike. Mine owners presented Captain Rynning with a gold watch for his efforts.

Roosevelt was always thereafter proud of his action in the Morenci strike. He spoke of the incident often and even included it in his autobiography. He appears to have been blinded by the need for vindication. After gaining a reputation as a friend of labor by his intercession in the 1902 eastern coal strike, the new president seems to have been anxious to prove that he was actually neutral. The Morenci strike gave him the chance to demonstrate that he could be tough on labor too, should it be in the wrong. That accomplished, Roosevelt was unconcerned with any details.

At the very time that Acting Governor Stoddard was attempting to cope with the emergency in Morenci, he may have been the subject of some discussion between President Roosevelt and Governor Brodie. An investigation had been made and charges had been prepared against Stoddard. Now these charges were before the President. These stemmed from the stubborn fight Stoddard was waging to continue receiving extravagant income from incorporation of businesses in

Arizona. In fighting the Cowan Bill, Stoddard was alleged to have "maintained a corrupt and unscrupulous lobby," essentially attempting to bribe legislators. After the bill passed, Stoddard still struggled to keep his privileged income. Another charge was falsifying records and a third was destruction of his records.

By the following spring, Stoddard sought the help of New York party boss Platt to negotiate his resignation in return for a statement by the President or the Attorney General that "the charges filed against Stoddard by individuals in Arizona have either been disproved or have not been substantiated by the evidence submitted." Roosevelt refused the condition and demanded Stoddard's resignation. In return the President would consider the matter closed and make no statement. [45]Secretary Stoddard accepted these conditions.

Governor Brodie also succeeded in delivering an Arizona delegation pledged to Roosevelt for the upcoming 1904 Republican National Convention. This was not unexpected. Those Republicans, opposed to the growing dominance of the Roosevelt wing in Arizona, could rightfully complain that the President did seem to have an unfair advantage. Though the territories could not be involved in the general election, they did send delegates to the party conventions. This was cause of some concern, especially because an incumbent president might be able to control the delegations from the territories through the broad power he had over patronage in the territories. If the territory had elected a congressional delegate from the same party as the president, and that delegate had been given the power over patronage customary for the position, the party leaders might have more autonomy in their instructions to convention delegates. But with the congressional delegate from the opposite party of the president, as in 1904 Arizona,

---

45 Roosevelt further stated that this would be the best thing for Stoddard. Surprisingly Stoddard's political career in Arizona was not completely destroyed. He became a serious contender for appointment as Arizona's last territorial governor.

the president might appoint only his most loyal supporters to high government position, thereby putting those supporters in position to dominate the party and dictate the delegation to the national convention and other instructions.

Victory for the Roosevelt forces in Arizona was not, however, inevitable. The mainstream Arizona Republicans who had led the party in the days before Roosevelt declared in the *Arizona Republican* in mid-February that they would make a fight for control of the Arizona delegation. Governor Brodie believed that the President had earned the support of the Arizona delegation by first pushing the Newlands Irrigation Act through Congress, then choosing Arizona as the site of the first major project under that law, though this choice could have very little political payoff due to Arizona's politically impotent territorial status. The anti-Brodie forces pointed out that they were not really anti-Roosevelt. They wanted to send an Arizona delegation uncommitted to any candidate. Privately they had to have been upset with Roosevelt for having reduced them to secondary roles behind Republicans of dubious loyalty to the party, many of whom did not contribute financially to the party and some of whom were recently converted former Democrats. Outwardly, they criticized Roosevelt as a promoter of joint statehood, thereby, distancing themselves from the President on this issue.

After allowing the Arizona governor the freedom to disagree with him on the key issue of joint statehood, Roosevelt could reasonably expect that the governor would deliver a delegation for him to the convention, not withstanding any opposition. Governor Brodie was able to produce. The Arizona delegation, which included new Republican Benjamin Daniels, was instructed for Roosevelt, and the governor was chosen unanimously to lead the delegation. At the territorial convention Brodie accepted the leadership of the delegation, saying, "It will be one of the happiest days of my life when I cast my vote for Theodore Roosevelt."

Governor Brodie had become a power in his own right in Arizona and a more nearly equal partner of the President in issues involving Arizona. While he and Arizona could support the President completely on most issues, he could also challenge the President, as on the joint statehood proposal. The same Arizona territorial convention which authorized a Roosevelt delegation to the Republican National Convention passed an "anti-carpetbagger rule." When Isaac Stoddard finally resigned, the President wrote to Brodie that he might have to appoint a New York friend of Stoddard to succeed him as secretary for political reasons. Brodie's objection caused the President to reconsider and appoint an Arizonan to the post.

In September, the prison superintendent position came open again. The scheme which Roosevelt and Brodie had planned two years earlier, but which Brodie had later abandoned for fear of political repercussions, was now implemented. The governor quietly appointed Ben Daniels. Apparently, no strong opposition was heard though Daniels' prison experience was unique for a superintendent.

All the surviving Rough Rider officers from Arizona's three troops were doing well in 1904, and many were in government service. Some who had been politically active Democrats were now, or would soon become, the new breed "Roosevelt Republicans." Democrat Frank Frantz was appointed postmaster of Enid, Oklahoma shortly after being mustered out of the army. Two years later he became agent to the Osage Indians of Oklahoma. Joshua D. Carter, always popular in Prescott, served as undersheriff of Yavapai County before he was appointed secretary of the Livestock Sanitation Board. George Wilcox, who had been unsuccessful in his campaign for territorial council in 1898, was elected justice of the peace in 1900. This man, whom Roosevelt called "the best among the Arizonans," was soon after rewarded with a very well-paying position as clerk of the district court of Tombstone, though he was a prominent Democrat at the time. C Troop's Captain J. L. B. Alexander had a successful private law practice in Phoenix and was still considered to be among the important leaders of the Democratic Party, though Arizona newspapers were speculating about a possible change in loyalties. James McClintock, as was mentioned earlier, was the postmaster of Phoenix and a colonel in the Arizona National Guard. Robert S. Patterson, formerly of Safford, Arizona, was making his own political fortunes as a Democrat, having been elected mayor of Yuma. Tom Rynning, of course, was the Ranger captain.

The Rough Riders and their Colonel were providing Arizona with a few good citizens to lead the territory toward statehood, and the federal government, with the President's encouragement, had begun a project to provide a little badly needed water.

CHAPTER 5

The Double Burden, 1905–1909

I have the distinction of never holding any official position under the Roosevelt administration, and that puts me in a class by myself as far as this regiment is involved. I've held no official position and never been in jail.

—James C. Goodwin
Member Arizona House of Representatives
Former Rough Rider, 1910

Theodore Roosevelt's 1904 rout of Democratic candidate Judge Alton D. Parker was the most one-sided presidential election since 1820. In the east, Roosevelt carried every northern state while his opponent carried every former Confederate state and two border states, Kentucky and Maryland.[46] This, of course, already put Roosevelt well ahead of Parker because

---

46 Roosevelt had actually defeated Parker by fewer than one hundred popular votes out of 220,000 votes cast in Maryland, but because of gerrymandering Roosevelt was awarded one electoral vote to seven for Parker in that state.

of the greater population of the north, but the west provided the crushing blow. Every state west of the Mississippi River except Texas and Louisiana went to Roosevelt. The love affair between the Rough Rider and the west was in full blossom.

The joint statehood issue, however, complicated Roosevelt's relationship with Arizona and destroyed the political career of Governor Brodie. During the contest to secure Arizona's Republican delegation for Roosevelt's nomination, Brodie promised that Roosevelt did not favor the merger of Arizona and New Mexico. Roosevelt, who vacillated on the issue of jointure, announced his support for the plan early in 1905. Now Brodie's detractors criticized the governor for deliberate deception. While he had been a popular governor, he was now discredited and forced from office. His term was about to expire anyway, and a second term for an appointed territorial governor was unusual at that time.

The Rough Rider governor left office on these disagreeable terms, but he had established a very respectable record. He had opposed the domination of the territory by the mines and had tried, albeit unsuccessfully, to convince the legislature to tax the mines more than a token amount. He had saved the territory a great deal of money by pushing through the legislature the bill to have corporate filing fees paid to the territorial treasury, rather than to the territorial secretary. He had consistently advocated federal sponsorship of dam projects in Arizona, and he deserves some of the credit for obtaining federal funds for Roosevelt Dam (then under construction). Overall, he ran an efficient administration which was never tainted by any hint of corruption. But now he needed a job.

Roosevelt rewarded Brodie for his extraordinary devotion with the position of assistant chief of the Records and Pensions Bureau of the army as a regular army major. How exciting this must have been for the old West Pointer after so many disappointments and so many years. His enlistment as a private soldier after resigning his commission had been unfulfilling. Commanding the Arizona National Guard was apparently unsatisfying. Command of the Arizona Rough Rider squadron was brief. And intercession on his behalf by Roosevelt had been fruitless while Roosevelt was New York governor and vice president.

Governor Brodie resigned on February 14, 1905 while the twenty-third legislature was in session. In his address to the legislature on January 5, he noted that two important projects were proceeding in Arizona under the National Reclamation Act. Theodore Roosevelt Dam on the Salt River was the big project. The other was Laguna Dam on the Colorado. The governor also repeated the often-heard plea for greater taxation of the fabulously wealthy mines. Even in his last week in office, Alexander Brodie tended carefully to business and advocated careful use of government funds. When the twenty-third legislature began appointing an unusual number of clerks and assistants, he called a conference of the leaders of both houses and, as a result, the support staff was trimmed considerably. Governor Brodie was held in such high regard that the Democratic controlled legislature issued a "resolution of esteem" and presented him with a saber when he left office.

The governor's secretary and speech writer, George Smalley, later reflected:

> Governor Brodie was a most lovable character. He was very popular in the territory with Democrats as well as Republicans. His administration was distinguished for honesty and integrity throughout. He was keenly interested in anything pertaining to advancement of the Territory and the happiness of its people.

Even the dynamic and very partisan Democrat George W. P. Hunt was favorably impressed by Brodie. According to Hunt's biographer, John S. Goff, Hunt "had great admiration" for Governor Brodie. Goff also writes, "Rarely did Hunt have much of anything good to say for a Republican, but Brodie won his praise as one the 'big interests could never buy.'"

Arizona's ex-governor had only one ceremonial task to perform before leaving civilian life behind. His friend Theodore Roosevelt had asked him to select and lead the Rough Rider honor guard in the presidential inauguration of 1905. Brodie selected thirty men to represent all the various parts of the country where Rough Riders had been recruited. He designated six fellow Arizonans to be included: three captains, McClintock and Alexander, and Frantz, who had been promoted on the death of O'Neill; First Lieutenant George Wilcox; and two enlisted men, Ben Daniels and C. E. Mills, the mine superintendent who was "too good a private" to be an

officer. Roosevelt obviously held these Rough Riders in very high regard. Included in the schedule of the President of the United States on inauguration night 1905 was a private reception for his colorful cowboy honor guard.

Roosevelt took some time choosing a successor for Governor Brodie. When the latter left office the position was briefly vacant. In filling the post, the President seemed unconcerned with the wishes of Arizona's Republican Party regulars. He wanted to get someone he knew personally and in whom he had confidence. He briefly considered appointing Democrat George Wilcox. Somehow the Tombstone *Prospector* discovered this and reported that Governor Brodie had endorsed Wilcox, and he would be Arizona's next governor if he wanted the job. Wilcox immediately denied that he had been contacted by either TR or Brodie about the job. The *Prospector* was, however, correct in pointing out that Wilcox's earnings as clerk of the court in Tombstone were much greater than the governor's salary. The pay difference would have been a major disincentive for Wilcox to change jobs. Roosevelt consulted with Brodie and finally named Joseph H. Kibbey on

Brodie's recommendation. Kibbey was a prominent progressive Republican.

Shortly after his 1905 inauguration, President Roosevelt was on his way to the fourth Rough Rider reunion in San Antonio. He was at first unexcited by, and perhaps even apprehensive of, his speaking tour of Texas, a state which had rejected him by a better than two-to-one majority in the November election. He wrote to John Hay on April 2, "I leave tomorrow for a week's horrid anguish in touring Kentucky, Indian Territory, and Texas...." However, a friendly welcome in Kentucky and genuine enthusiasm in the Lone Star State surprised and delighted him. At one dinner in his honor attended by some two hundred Texas businessmen, the President was given silver spurs with golden rowels symbolizing that "he had won his spurs" as "more than a middling good Democrat" in the words of the presenter.

The Rough Rider theme of this presidential tour, with its emphasis on San Antonio and the glory of San Juan Hill, gave it an atmosphere of refocused, inclusive nationalism. Roosevelt was soon cautiously optimistic about Texas. On April 8 he wrote to William Howard Taft about his experience in Texas:

> I have had a great reception in Texas, these mercurial people have gone to great lengths of wild enthusiasm in the revulsion of finding out that I really have no dark and sinister designs against their liberties and general welfare. The reception probably means nothing at all, but it may possibly mean a little better general feeling and a little more likelihood of an occasional Texas vote for some measure of interest to the general welfare of the nation, such as Santo Domingo, or Panama, or the Philippines. At any rate it is a good thing that I came. I really like the Texans....

The positive reception given to the President in Texas inspired his two-week grand tour of the south later that fall, during which he was accompanied by Rough Riders John McIlhenny of Louisiana and John C. Greenway formerly of Hot Springs, Arkansas.

At the San Antonio reunion, Charles Hunter, a sergeant of D Troop, the New Mexicans attached to the Arizona squadron, became the first enlisted man to be elected president of the Rough Rider Association. Roosevelt also spoke with his newly appointed Arizona governor. Governor Kibbey came as a special guest and extended an invitation to the President to attend the dedication of the Buckey O'Neill statue in Prescott in 1907. Roosevelt accepted this invitation and the association members resolved to meet next in Prescott at the dedication with the understanding that "the colonel" would be there.

"The colonel" was more than casually interested and involved with affairs in Arizona, especially when those affairs concerned his favorites from among his regiment. In 1905, three Arizona Rough Riders received appointments to prominent positions. Henry Bardshar, who had been the colonel's orderly, became collector of internal revenue for Arizona and New Mexico. Captain Joseph L. B. Alexander of C Troop, a newly converted "Roosevelt Republican," accepted an appointment as US attorney for Arizona. Among the recommendation in his 1905 appointment file is one from Marcus Smith, Arizona's leading Democrat, who was probably grinning about the choice of his old Democratic colleague. More surprisingly still Roosevelt once again appointed Benjamin Daniels as US marshal. The faith which Roosevelt put in Daniels, even after he had lied and embarrassed the President, is not easy to understand. On the other hand, if Roosevelt was right in his perception of Daniels as a loyal friend, the lawman might take very seriously what his colonel called the "double burden" of the Rough Riders in office "to make the best kind of record" first for themselves as individuals, then for the regiment. By the time of this appointment, Daniels had been prison superintendent for eight months and, judging from the letters of reference he was able to obtain, he had done a good to excellent job running the prison.

Roosevelt was much more cautious and clever with the appointment this time than he had been in 1902. Now Myron McCord had finished his full term. The appointment was well timed in another way too. It was made while Congress was out of session. Daniels would be a sitting marshal with a record to examine when the time came for the Senate to confirm his appointment. In the meantime, Roosevelt carefully gathered endorsements of his candidate along with explanations of previous charges. He presented these to the members of the Senate Judiciary Committee in advance. The confirmation was still not easy. The Senate committee delayed the approval almost a year until May 1906, at which time they voted unanimously to confirm the appointment.

The only controversy involving Daniels that first year was the result of a communications breakdown between him and the incoming prison superintendent. Famed Arizona outlaw Burt Alvord was serving time at the Yuma prison when Daniels resigned as superintendent to take the marshal job. In the fall of 1905, officials in Sonora, Mexico requested custody of Alvord on the completion of his sentence on October 25. Daniels may have been slow in delivering the request, but he knew Alvord's scheduled release time. The new superintendent, Jerry Millay, however, released Alvord three weeks early. The outlaw thus escaped Mexican justice. Alvord's Tombstone lawyer, Thomas E. Flanningan, had publicly stated that Alvord would not be turned over to Mexico and that the details of Alvord's release had been arranged. Federal investigator, J. D. Harris, reviewed the case and exonerated Daniels while accusing Millay of "gross negligence." No criminal charges were filed. As an interesting side note, Alvord soon fled to Mexico refusing to pay his attorney fees.

When Ben Daniels took over as marshal from McCord, he found at least three Rough Rider comrades employed as deputies—David Hughes, Charles Utting, and John Foster. He soon hired three other Rough Rider deputies, Walter Gregory, who had been his secretary at the prison, Thomas Mooney, and Samuel Greenwald. Greenwald, who had been a sergeant in the regiment, impressed Roosevelt in the big battle at San Juan Heights. Roosevelt had Greenwald commissioned as a second lieutenant soon after. Greenwald apparently, however, could not adjust to the deputy job. He resigned within a month. David Hughes also resigned in September. Remarkably, of these Rough Rider deputies, only Mooney remained in the marshal service after the first year of Ben Daniels' command, and Daniels hired no other Rough Riders. Records show Walter Gregory to have been very active and conscientious. He resigned after ten months to accept a position as postmaster of Sierra Madre, California.

Marshal Daniels was a good friend of Ranger Captain Tom Rynning and US Attorney J. L. B. Alexander. The friendship of these three men, forged during their Cuban service, facilitated coordinated efforts targeting specific criminal activity. Close association between the marshal's office and the Rangers had already occurred under Marshal McCord. McCord had instituted the policy of cross deputizing three Rangers as deputy marshals. McCord and Rynning had also cultivated a cordial working relationship with Colonel Emilio Kosterlitzky, the romantic Russian-born commander of the rurales, who patrolled northern Mexico. Daniels maintained these connections and worked at improving them.

The proximity of the Mexican border had always posed special problems for law enforcement in Arizona. One of the reasons for the formation of the Rangers had been that large numbers of cattle had been stolen in southern Arizona and herded across the border. The border also provided sanctuary for Arizona fugitives and a source of access for unwanted, illegal Chinese aliens. To these problems was added Mexico's volatile political situation in the early twentieth century which threatened to involve the United States.

Mexico allowed posses from Arizona to cross the border in hot pursuit and Arizona reciprocated, but cooperation along the border was much more extensive than just that. One example of this cooperation involved the then famous disappearance in Mexico of a party led by Douglas School Superintendent Thomas Grindell, the Rough Rider and former English professor who had run for school superintendent in Maricopa County in 1898. In the early autumn of 1905 Colonel Kosterlitzky invited Captain Rynning and a few other Rangers along on an expedition to locate the remains of these Americans who were known to have been on the west coast of Mexico north of Guaymas and were presumed dead.

Grindell and his small band of heavily armed men intended to explore the island of Tiburon off the coast of Mexico. Natives of the island were rumored to practice cannibalism, but the island was thought to be rich in gold. Grindell had visited the island the summer before. The group took an ill-conceived land route south though a long stretch of desert and apparently ran out of water. The only survivor stated that he became separated from the group near the coast with the island just across the channel, and he survived by distilling water. They had no boats to take them to the island because the coastal town where they had expected to purchase boats was found deserted.

Kosterlitzky, Rynning, and party searched the coast and found a campsite of the Grindell party containing equipment, ammunition, and the remains of pack animals. The search party also chartered a boat which navigated around the island, but the captain and crew refused to land on the island fearing the inhabitants. The bodies of the explorers were never recovered, but their friends and families could be assured that the governments of Mexico and Arizona had done all they could in the matter.

The cordial relations at the border were severely strained the following year by a strike at an American owned copper mine at Cananea, Mexico. Wages at the mine were lower than at similar mines north of the border but higher than general wage levels in Mexico. The greatest source of difficulty was that a rigid caste system prevailed with Anglo-Americans in nearly all the administrative, supervisorial, and otherwise higher paying jobs. The mine at Cananea employed about 6,000 Mexicans and 600 Anglo-Americans. The Mexican strikers demanded a raise from three to five pesos per day, a workday shortened from ten to eight hours, and that half of the foremen be Mexicans. "Colonel" William Greene, the mine owner, portrayed the Cananea strike as a racial conflict between two armed factions with the Anglo-American faction vastly outnumbered and in danger of annihilation.

John Kenneth Turner, an American socialist who supported the Mexican liberation movement, accused Greene of manipulating American public opinion to gain armed intervention against the strikers. This charge has some justification. If an unusually dangerous situation did exist, it seems to have been provoked by the Americans. As the strike began, the miners quickly seized the entire works except for the lumberyard. When a large number of miners approached the lumberyard peacefully to speak with the workers there, the American supervisor, George Metcalf, soaked them with a fire hose. While Metcalf did warn his victims first, the incident inflamed the atmosphere instantly, because most of the strikers were wearing their Sunday clothes.[47] According

---

47 C. L. Sonnichsen, *Colonel Greene and the Copper Skyrocket,* (Tucson: The University of Arizona Press, 1974): 182-183.

to Turner, the strikers were not armed, but threw stones at the lumberyard defenders, George Metcalf and his brother William, in response to their drenching. Turner claims that the Americans then escalated the conflict by firing rifles at the strikers and the strikers then overpowered and killed the two brothers. One of the brothers was killed with miners' tools, not gunfire. This would appear to substantiate the contention that the miners involved in this episode had few arms. At least three Mexicans were killed, and others wounded by gunfire in the confrontation. Turner exaggerated when he claimed that the miners were completely unarmed, but the fact that they were dressed in their best clothes seems to indicate that they did not intend or expect to fight.

The incident in the lumberyard prompted Greene to telephone Bisbee frantically begging for help since Kosterlitzky's rurales were not in the vicinity. According to Greene, help was needed immediately to avoid a massacre of the entire Anglo-American community. By coincidence, Captain Rynning was in Bisbee when Greene called. Many excited citizens of Bisbee quickly prepared to go to Cananea to support the Americans there. Rynning jumped ahead of the situation and organized the volunteers.

They rode a train south to the border where they met Governor Yzabal of Sonora. Arizona Governor Kibbey sent three telegrams to Captain Rynning ordering him not to cross the border, but, guessing the contents, the Ranger captain had the telegrams intercepted by his subordinates who were conveniently unable to find him. A quick compromise was reached with the Sonoran governor allowing the Americans to cross the border as individuals rather than as a group. Once they were in Mexico, the Sonora governor swore in the Americans as volunteer militiamen, and they boarded another

---

To make matters worse, George Metcalf was generally unpopular with the Mexican workers for his rigidity as housing director of the company.

—

train to Cananea. Arriving about 11:00 a.m., Rynning ordered most of his men to deploy on the high ground outside the town. Colonel Greene soon appeared on a platform and spoke to the strikers, trying to calm them down.

That Colonel Greene dared to expose himself at this time indicates the situation may not have been as threatening as he had claimed. The fact that the deployment of a mere three hundred armed Americans quieted the strikers also suggests that the Mexicans were poorly armed. The results of the gun battles which had occurred before Rynning arrived also suggest the same conclusion. Casualty figures from the fighting and photographs taken during the strike indicate that American defenders were well armed while Mexican strikers had few guns. A total of only five Americans died while official Mexican government figures claimed twenty-six Mexican strikers killed. Most sources agree that the number of Mexican dead was much larger than the official figure.

About 6:00 p.m., the rurales arrived. Kosterlitzky was at first angry, or at least unhappy, to see the Americans. But Rynning allowed the Russian to control the situation in the town, and Kosterlitzky was probably happy to have the support in cowing the strikers once he realized that Rynning would not interfere with his authority.

Later, when Governor Kibbey confronted Rynning about the incident, Kibbey supposedly said, "You deserve to be severely punished for what you have done and I will try to make the punishment fit the crime— how would you like to be superintendent of the prison?"

The longtime Ranger captain did, in fact, become the next superintendent of the territorial prison which, we will see, offered a truly unique challenge at that time, perfectly matched to Rynning's qualifications. Roosevelt was not unhappy about the infringement of Mexican sovereignty. When he was told of the Cananea episode, he is reported to have commented, "Tom's all right, isn't he?" The Sonoran governor's actions did not meet with such sympathy by his government. He was replaced.

We cannot easily fault Rynning's actions in the strike. Bisbee volunteers would have gone to Cananea with or without his leadership. If Rynning had not been involved, a disorganized mob might have created an international incident at the border, or many lives might have been lost in needless, bloody confrontations with strikers or rurales. The resulting situation would certainly have turned out no better without him and may have been much worse. The physical danger to Americans was probably real enough, though the actual cause of the crisis is debatable.

Colonel Greene may have believed that the Cananea strike was linked to a general liberation movement which was beginning in Mexico at that time. That some strike leaders sought the expulsion of American businesses from Mexico is probable; that the average striker at Cananea considered himself a revolutionary is more doubtful.

Not only did the revolutionary movement threaten US investment in Mexico, but it also threatened to involve the United States in war, because Mexican dissidents used the United States as a staging base for operations in Mexico. During the years 1906 and 1907 the marshal's office, the Rangers, and the US attorney's office coordinated many efforts to root out Mexican dissidents operating in southern Arizona. President Roosevelt blessed and encouraged these efforts. A group of dissidents calling themselves the "Liberty Club" had established a headquarters in Douglas, Arizona. In September 1906, Rangers under Captain Rynning raided that headquarters, arrested seven men, and confiscated explosives. The *Arizona Republican* reported that Rynning acted "in the capacity of deputy marshal," and that the US attorney's office had issued warrants for several other Mexicans. These warrants resulted in two more arrests. The Rangers also arrested three other leaders of the revolutionary movement in the Patagonia Mountains north of Nogales, Arizona. All were charged with violation of neutrality laws of the United States and the Mexican citizens, who were the majority of those arrested, were threatened with deportation. The *Republican* also noted that the charges were brought at the request of the Mexican government. This gives credence to another accusation made by J. K. Turner, that the government of Porfirio Diaz dictated the policies of Arizona law enforcement.

Extreme precautions were taken to ensure the security of the three prisoners in Nogales because rumors floated that fellow revolutionaries would attempt to break them out of jail. Extra deputies were appointed to guard the prisoners, and they were taken to a more secure facility in Tucson as quickly as possible. Interest in these and other revolutionaries in and around Nogales caused seventy-five rurale cavalrymen on the other side of the border to make a forced march seventy-five miles to Nogales, Mexico, during which one cavalryman actually died from the hardship of the trip.

In the trial of the would-be revolutionaries, held in December, evidence suggested a plan to attack the town and mine of Cananea and, thereby, accomplish the goal of ousting Americans from control of the Mexican mine, which may have been vaguely in the minds of some of the strikers the year before. The Liberty Party leader, Tomas Espinosa, was sentenced to two years in prison at Yuma. Most of the others were turned over to Mexican authorities, and some of these were executed without legal recourse.

These men reputedly belonged to a larger organization headquartered in St. Louis, Missouri. When the office of that organization was contacted, Manuel Sarabia, a leader there, stated, "Neither our party in St. Louis nor our paper advocates anything like the methods reported in the Arizona dispatch. We approve working for great reforms in Mexico but want only the ballot and labor strike power used, and not force or anything in the way of rebellion." This is noteworthy because Sarabia would be in Douglas the next year, and there, would become the victim of what Turner called the "most notable case of refugee kidnapping on record."

That incident involved the marshal's office, the Rangers, the Mexican government, and, by a strange twist, "Mother" Jones, the famous union organizer. Sarabia had been arrested and jailed without charge in Douglas in June 1907. The night of his arrest he was taken from the Douglas jail, transported by automobile to the border, and turned over to Mexican authorities. While being forced into the car in Douglas, Sarabia managed to yell out that he was being kidnapped. Several people heard him and alerted local newspapers and Mother Jones, who was in Douglas that night to support union activities.

As Mother Jones later related, she at first did not take the report of the abduction seriously. After she was convinced that something unusual did happen, she ordered immediate telegrams to Governor Kibbey and President Roosevelt. "We got Teddy out of bed that night," she told a union audience years later. The next day she organized a rally in Douglas to inform the citizens about the abduction and to organize a protest. The Western Federation of Miners, whom Mother Jones represented, took a special interest in the Mexican dissidents after this, contributing to their legal defense on several occasions. The campaign to free Sarabia may have saved his life. He was returned to Arizona eight days after his abduction. True to his earlier statement in St. Louis, his activities in Arizona had been confined to writing for radical newspapers. He was allowed to go free, while some of his abductors were charged, but none were convicted. The Rangers and the marshal's office were both implicated in the abduction, but little investigation was done. Conflict between the marshal's office and the dissidents continued and peaked in a sensational trial in early 1909.

Mother Jones stopped by Phoenix on her way north to other union business and spoke with Governor Kibbey and the new Ranger Captain Harry Wheeler. She was favorably impressed by both. Her impressions were soon to be tested because a major strike was already in progress in Bisbee. This Arizona governor resisted the demands of mine operators for National Guard troops, but he did send the Arizona Rangers to keep the peace. In that role Captain Wheeler won praise from all sides for impartial enforcement of the law without military reinforcements. Unnecessary use of military force on the side of management, common in western labor disputes, would not happen in this strike. To Kibbey's credit, he changed that pattern in Arizona, and the cool, responsible, fair handedness of Captain Wheeler contributed to the change. The strike was long. It lasted from April 10 until December 27. The union was defeated in the end, but it had gained the right to strike by proving that it could strike peacefully, given reasonably impartial law enforcement.

Had Governor Brodie held office in 1907, he might have sacrificed fairness for expedience. He had chosen to ignore the injustice which destroyed the union in Morenci in 1903. Brodie was heavily influenced by Roosevelt who hated the Western Federation of Miners, the dominant union in the west at the time. The President once called three of its most prominent leaders "undesirable citizens" at a time when these three were on trial for conspiracy to commit murder. Governor Kibbey had the advantage of not being so close to the forceful Rough Rider as to lose his independent perspective.

Roosevelt's Rough Rider patronage in Arizona had mixed effects. Men who knew, liked, and trusted each other carried out presidential policies in a unified and efficient manner. Brodie's friendship with Roosevelt facilitated direct communication with the President. And personal loyalty to Roosevelt encouraged high standards of conduct by office holders who were careful not to do anything to injure or embarrass the President. However, Roosevelt's dominant personality submerged most dissenting opinions among these men. They accepted Roosevelt's priorities without question and allocated resources accordingly. These priorities included uprooting the Mexican dissidents, including the desperate Yaqui Indians, stopping illegal Chinese immigration through Mexico, and opposing the Western Federation of Miners.

By the midway point in Roosevelt's second term, Roosevelt backers and appointees in Arizona were becoming increasingly isolated, not only from mainstream Arizonans, who were typically Democrats, but also from fellow Republicans. The joint statehood issue insured that "Roosevelt Republicans" would remain on the fringe of Arizona's Republican Party. The issue, at the same time, wounded mainstream Republicans. By 1906, the President probably realized that if the union was to be completed during his administration fast action was necessary. And pressure from the territories and their advocates mounted. But the one strong argument of Senator Beveridge against the independent admission of both Arizona and New Mexico still made sense. Populations in the two territories were still small, particularly in Arizona. To admit these two states and their four senators would further imbalance representation in the Senate, increasing the likelihood that a small minority of people would decide national issues against the will of the vast majority.

In addition to this, the political implications for the Republican Party nationally were much better with joint statehood. The voting population of New Mexico was much larger than that of Arizona, and New Mexico was politically split with a slight Republican leaning. A joint state—"Arizona the Great" Senator Beveridge called it— might elect two Republican senators. If not that, it would probably split with one senator from each party. The worst-case scenario, which was not likely, would be that two Democrats would be elected. But with separate statehood, Arizona would be expected to elect two Democratic senators, which meant that the best the GOP could hope with these two states would be to maintain its current position by electing two Republican senators in New Mexico. Roosevelt continued to endorse the joint statehood scheme through 1906.

The arguments made sense if joint statehood could be imposed upon Arizona against the will of its people. Roosevelt's endorsement alienated Arizonans. This left the mainstream Arizona Republicans, who already felt shut out by the administration, discredited and with the difficult job of damage control related to a policy to which most were essentially opposed themselves. "Roosevelt Republicans" in Arizona became increasingly dependent on Roosevelt's national influence which was bound to decline noticeably as soon as he left the White House. Finally, what Roosevelt did not know at that time was that by sacrificing his Arizona supporters in 1906, he contributed to his own defeat in "the baby state" in his 1912 attempt to regain the White House.

This costly effort actually nearly succeeded. Senator Beveridge pushed the joint statehood bill through Congress in 1906. Ironically, one of the leading opponents of the proposal in Arizona was Governor Kibbey, who had been appointed by Roosevelt, but was spearheading a coordinated effort by both parties to stop jointure. The outraged Senator Beveridge asked the President for Kibbey's removal, but Roosevelt refused. Senator Joseph Foraker, an Ohio Republican who became a formidable Roosevelt opponent, offered an amendment to the joint statehood bill which seemed fair but was sure to kill the measure. He pro-posed that the bill would have to be voted on in both territories and a majority in each territory would have to agree to the bill for it to become law. The amendment was adopted and the outcome was almost a forgone conclusion given the sentiment in Arizona. Though joint statehood passed in New Mexico, it failed by an overwhelming 16,265 to 3,141 in Arizona. Arizona had soundly rejected President Roosevelt's own personal appeal for support on the issue. This may have had some influence on his decision not to visit the territory that next summer as he had previously promised.

By coincidence two prominent Rough Rider memorials were both dedicated in 1907. Mrs. Allyn Capron, widow of the first Rough Rider officer killed in Cuba, led the Rough Riders' National Monument Society. It had erected a monument in Arlington National Cemetery, dedicated on April 12. Roosevelt attended this dedication, but despite his promise two years earlier, did not come to Prescott for the unveiling and dedication of the "Buckey O'Neill Monument." He stayed home at Oyster Bay. Without the colonel the proposed reunion at Prescott was canceled. The citizens of Prescott had to have been disappointed, but they were not disheartened as they prepared to celebrate a beautiful piece of art representing an admired local hero.

With the help of funds provided by the Territory of Arizona and many private contributions, they had erected the O'Neill Rough Rider Monument which is still the impressive centerpiece of the county square park of downtown Prescott across the street from Whiskey Row, where the famed Arizonan had spent much of his time (and money) "bucking the tiger." The respected sculptor Solon Borglum, working in New York, designed the figure of a horse and rider which Prescott's *Weekly Journal-Miner* described as follows:

> ...gallant captain, mounted on a charger. With distended nostrils the horse stands, slightly reared back on the haunches, as though abruptly pulled up, while his rider, with face turned towards the left,

sits in an attitude of expectancy, as though awaiting orders. It is a beautiful piece of craftsmanship; one well worth its subject.

The cavalryman depicted was not intended to resemble O'Neill or any other single individual, but rather to capture the spirit of O'Neill and the Rough Riders, which it still does well more than one hundred years later. It is mounted on a twenty-eight-ton boulder quarried from the nearby mountains.

Without Roosevelt and without the official designation of a Rough Rider reunion, the Fourth of July celebration in Prescott in 1907 was still a huge success, because it was not about Roosevelt; it was about O'Neill. The daughter of a prominent Prescott citizen and Buckey O'Neill's adopted son together unveiled the statue. Speeches were presented by Governor Kibbey, Associate Justice Sloan, and James McClintock, who represented both the National Guard and the Rough Riders. A parade was held featuring territorial dignitaries, the Arizona National Guard, and, of course, the Rough Riders. Those of the regiment in attendance included hometown boys Joshua Carter, Anton Johnson, Thomas Laird, and Orlando Byrnes. Some of the other Rough Riders who also attended were US Attorney Alexander, George Truman, J. M. McCoy, James C. Goodwin, and N. A. Vyne. The *Weekly Journal-Miner* published an attractive special edition in honor of the occasion, which quickly sold out by advanced orders. The second edition of 2,000 copies was printed and all but 500 of those were also sold in advance of publication. Interestingly, by 1907 the people of Prescott did not need Theodore Roosevelt to make this celebration meaningful; he was not important. In a timeless way, they still had, and still have, Buckey O'Neill. The Spanish-American War, however, was becoming old history and the gallantry of the Rough Riders probably seemed less relevant, even to the members of the regiment, as the nation passed into a new era. No more large reunions of the entire regiment would be held for many years.

Changing times then, as now, could always mean new opportunities. No other Rough Rider better symbolized the successful bridging of the nineteenth and twentieth centuries than did Tom Rynning in his role as prison superintendent. His administration of the Rangers has drawn mixed reviews by historians over the years. He did modernize the force and establish a level of professionalism unknown under Mossman. On the other hand, critics accused him of excessive use of force, intimidation tactics, and even disregard for the law, as in the Cananea strike and the Sarabia abduction. In 1907, he responded magnificently to a new challenge. With an initial appropriation of $120,000 and the authorization to use convict labor, Superintendent Rynning directed inmates in construction of a new prison at Florence to replace the infamous Yuma "Hell Hole." We should recall that he had operated a construction contracting business both before and after his service in the Spanish-American War. Superintendent Rynning was not involved in the planning of the structure, but rather in the day-to-day implementation of the architect's plans. Each convict was given two days off his sentence for each day of work. According to Rynning, the total cost of construction was held to $182,000 and the finished prison was appraised at $1,500,000. Rynning administered the prison very successfully. He served as superintendent for six years, 1906 to 1912. Then he went to San Diego where he became an undersheriff. In 1921, he returned to Arizona to accept appointment as prison superintendent again.

Ben Daniels also very successfully transformed himself into a modern marshal from the old-style lawman of the "old west." According to Larry Ball who has studied frontier law enforcement extensively, by the early twentieth century the sole function of US marshals in the east was to "serve the process of the federal court," but in the west the marshal's office took on additional duties of law enforcement which included federal investigation. At the same time Congress hesitated to authorize sufficient funds to cover the travel expenses of field deputies.[48] Despite the strain of limited resources and the complexity of the task unknown in the east, Daniels administered the marshal's office efficiently. The only charge of any consequence leveled against his administration was complicity in the Sarabia affair, and even that resulted from overzealousness, rather than laxity or self-interest. While Marshal Daniels did establish prosecution of neutrality violations on the border as a priority, he also diligently pursued illegal Chinese aliens funneled through Mexico and bootleggers selling liquor to the Indians.

He closely aligned his priorities with those of President Roosevelt.[49]

By the time Daniels had been marshal for a year, Roosevelt took great pride in the appointment. TR was, of course, always very enthusiastic about his Rough Riders. Nevertheless, his praise of Daniels is too glowing to be discounted. Counting the Arizona marshal among his best-appointed officials, Roosevelt wrote:

> ...thoroughly fearless, honest and intelligent administration of their respective offices by a large number of men such as...marshals like Ben Daniels in Arizona—and in short, a great variety of men who, in different positions, are all doing their duty and more than their duty with a hearty zeal and disinterested-ness.... When I look at the men I have named above

---

48 Larry D. Ball, *The United States Marshals of New Mexico and Arizona Territories, 1846–1912,* (Albuquerque: University of New Mexico, 1978): 219.

49 Interdiction by the marshal's office to stop the illegal entry of the Chinese aliens was so active as to cause US Attorney Alexander to seek the help of Representative Ralph Cameron to get an additional assistant. He reported 300 Chinese deported in the last year. J. L. B. Alexander to Hon. Ralph H. Cameron, July 14, 1909, Ralph Cameron Papers, Box 2 file 1, Special Collections, University of Arizona, Tucson.

and their like I feel we have got a pretty good country with pretty good men in it.

With all the Rough Riders who found their way into appointed government positions in the southwest, that very few proved to be unworthy is remarkable. One who apparently had serious problems was Fenn Hildredth, who had served as a private under James McClintock and had been appointed Register of the Land Office in Prescott. In July of 1905 he persuaded McClintock to write a strong letter to the President endorsing his work. In that letter McClintock wrote:

> …Hildredth's administration of the place of Register of the Prescott Land Office has been a most efficient one. I have been informed that the Commissioner of the General Land Office considers the Prescott office one of the best within his division…. The backing of practically all Northern Arizona is with Mr. Hildredth.

This may have been in reference to Hildredth's plan to consolidate the land offices in Prescott and Phoenix under his administration. A few months later McClintock sent a telegram to the President again endorsing Hildredth. Hildredth was facing resistance to his scheme. By March 1906, he confronted not only the Register of the Phoenix Land Office, whose job he wanted to take, but also the governor of Arizona. He accused Governor Kibbey of a conflict of interest as the former attorney for the Salt River Users' Association. No actual charges were leveled against the Governor. Nor were charges leveled against the rival register in Phoenix, but Hildredth asserted that he was senile and about to die from consumption.

Hildredth may have had financial difficulties which spurred him to desperation. Fellow Rough Rider and US Attorney J. L. B. Alexander had the unpleasant task of later investigating

Hildredth for embezzlement and arson. According to Alexander, Hildredth had been gambling in Phoenix and was in debt. The rented house in which he lived burned down at a very opportune time. He had just insured its contents at what Alexander estimated as double their value. On the night of the fire, he had taken his wife to a hotel. Given these facts, Alexander believed him guilty. Hildredth, however, does not appear to have been charged in connection with the fire and was never actually tried for anything. Alexander eventually charged Hildredth with two counts of embezzlement of federal funds, but these charges were dropped because the amounts were small. Despite all this, Hildredth had recovered his reputation enough by 1911 to be nominated for the Arizona Senate on the Republican ticket. At that time the *Arizona Republican* called Hildredth "a businessman who persists in staying at the top, in spite of adversity and hard luck."

Alexander had ordered the dismissal of the Hildredth case. The US Attorney in Arizona had bigger concerns than petty pilfering. He directed his attention to the Mexican border. Alexander's close friendship with Marshal Daniels facilitated their working toward com-mon goals. The two worked together on the Liberty Club case in 1906 and the subsequent trial, which occurred in 1909. The 1906 Grand Jury in Douglas ordered the arrest of the three members of the Mexican Liberty Party living in Los Angeles. The three—Ricardo Magnon, Antonio Villareal, and Librado Rivera—were taken into custody, but, backed by funding from the Western Federation of Miners, they fought extradition to Arizona in the courts. They had appealed to the United States Supreme Court but abandoned their plea in December 1908. On March 3, 1909, they were turned over to Marshal Daniels.

The Federal Government tried these accused revolutionaries in Tombstone with US Attorney Alexander pleading the government's case against them. During the course of the trial, vague threats were made against Alexander which caused Daniels to tighten security. The verdict of the trial was guilty, and the defendants were each sentenced to eighteen months in prison. J. K. Turner claims that this sentence was excessive. They had already been held in jail for over two years, and they had never actually attacked Mexico with anything other than words.

Actions taken against Mexican revolutionaries beg comparison to the sympathetic response Cubans, with the same general goals for their country, had received only a decade earlier. Viewed through this lens we see a great deal of irony in the actions of the former libera-tors of Cuba. Besides the private war waged on the Mexican radicals in Arizona, Marshal Daniels also worked diligently to stop the flow of guns to the Yaqui Indians who were resisting extermination just south of the border. Marshal Daniels was only doing his job and Roosevelt was enforcing American neutrality with regard to the affairs of another sovereign nation. Yet Roosevelt's callousness toward the plight of the Yaquis is inconsistent with the determination he showed to help the Cubans in 1898.

The simple pragmatic difference may have been that Cuba did not share a border with the United States and therefore, posed no threat. From the economic perspective we can say that in Cuba the US fought to establish a stable environment for American enterprise; in Mexico American enterprise was already dominant and would remain so if the status quo could be maintained. John Kenneth Turner calculated that Americans had 900 mil-lion dollars invested in Mexico in 1909 with 80% of Mexican exports going to the United States and 68% of Mexican imports coming from the states. Another source estimates American investment around 500 mil-lion dollars, still a huge amount for that time. Dollar diplomacy submerged idealism in America's dealings with Mexico.

Roosevelt also failed to understand the revolutionary movement in Mexico at that time. He perceived these dissidents as the Mexican equivalent to the fringe, and dangerous, anarchist movement in the United States. He respected Mexican dictator Porfirio Diaz. His profound misunderstanding of the Mexican situation is obvious in a letter he wrote in March 1908. In this he says: "I quite agree with you that Mexico's President Porfirio Diaz is the greatest statesman now living, and he has done for his country what no other living man has done for any other country—which is the supreme test of the value of a statesman."

Roosevelt approved and encouraged the aggressive prosecution of Mexican dissidents in Arizona. In June 1908 he specifically ordered the strict enforcement of American neutrality laws with regard to Mexican dissidents at the request of the Mexican government. In fairness to Roosevelt, we must note that the request resulted from an actual attack by dissidents on Mexico, crossing the Rio Grande from Texas. That such attacks never occurred on the Arizona-Mexico border might even be to the credit of such men as Rynning, Daniels, and Alexander. Roosevelt's response to the dissident problem was not idealistic, but it was with thought to American national interest and it was politically popular.

Roosevelt's trusted Rough Riders—Brodie, Alexander, Daniels, and Rynning—provided the President with what he wanted, efficient enforcement of his policies in Arizona. But they failed to provide him with information which might alter those policies, information he did not want, but needed.

CHAPTER 6

The Stand at Armageddon, 1909–1912

He (Roosevelt) had no need of him (God) and no longing, because he really had no need of anything but his own immensely sufficient self. And the abundant, crowding, magnificent presence of this world left no room for another.

—Gamaliel Bradford[50]

Just days after the defeat of the joint statehood resolution in November 1906, the *Arizona Republican* published a front-page cartoon of an Arizona Ranger standing over the body of "joint statehood," extending his hand in friendship to both President Roosevelt and House Speaker Joe Cannon, while an angry little Senator Beveridge looks on in the background. The caption read "Let's make up." The Republican paper naturally hoped for quick reconciliation. The editor interpreted the demeanor of Roosevelt correctly. The five-to-one defeat of the

---

50 Quoted in William Harbaugh, *The Life and Times of Theodore Roosevelt,* (London: Oxford University Press, 1975): 215.

—

joint statehood referendum in Arizona convinced the President that the people of Arizona would never accept joint statehood.

Unfortunately, statements made by Roosevelt during the joint statehood campaign prohibited him from support of immediate separate statehood for Arizona and New Mexico. He had warned in a public statement that:

> …it is my belief that if the people of Arizona let this chance go by they will have to wait very many years before the chance again offers itself, and then it will very probably be only upon the present terms—that is upon the condition of being joined with New Mexico.

On August 31, 1907, the President wrote to Governor Kibbey assuring him that no further actions would be taken by the administration toward joint statehood. Shortly after this, Roosevelt informed Senator Beveridge of this decision and added, "New Mexico ought to come in at once as a state. I am inclined to think it better to make it a complete job and bring in Arizona also." Roosevelt soon after conferred with congressional leaders in the hope that these states could still be brought in during his administration but was disappointed to hear from many that they now preferred to wait until after the 1910 census to determine the accuracy of recent claims of dramatic population increases in both territories. The President, consequently, refrained from making public statements regarding statehood for Arizona or New Mexico for over a year.

In 1908, the Arizona Republican Party grimly deter-mined to rebuild its fortunes with a long-term strategy. Republican congressional candidate Ralph Cameron campaigned very actively. But the rhetoric in the territory's leading Republican paper, the *Arizona Republican* of Phoenix, lacked the customary hype of "certain victory," substituting a surprising theme of respectability and resignation. The following remarks made in an October 6 article indicate the demoralized condition of the

Arizona GOP before the 1908 election and the limited goals and gains expected in that election:

> Chairman [Hovel] Smith, as well as all of his subordinates and assistants, is finding great pride in the fact that the republican [sic] organization throughout the territory, is better, stronger, and more unified than at any time in the past political history of the territory.... We all hope and trust that he [Cameron] will be elected, but every man concerned with the republican organization throughout the territory, is sufficiently broad minded and philosophical to accept defeat at the hands of the people, and all can find solace in the fact that if they are defeated there has at least, been built up an organization which means much for the immediate welfare of all the people....
>
> To prophesy political success in the face of past political experience and history in this territory, as between republicans and democrats, in a squarely fought contest, would not become any republican of intelligence at this time, because such a prophecy would be the usurpation of good sense by optimism.

In the article quoted above, the *Republican* also announced that Republican leaders would not attack the character of Democratic opponents like Mark Smith. Character was not particularly important in this election according to Republicans. Nor was personality. Again according to the *Republican*, personality "in the mind of every intelligent voter, should have no bearing whatever, in deciding how to vote."

Voters were reminded of "the simple fact...that either of them [Smith or Cameron] if elected will be nothing but a public official...naught but public servants." *Republican* argued for Cameron on practical ground:

> Mark Smith has been tried for eighteen years; and it can
> be said without any dis-credit to him either as a man,
> or his ability as a man among men, that he cannot and
> has not been able to do the work the people wish done,
> because the conditions confronting him have been such
> that no man similarly situated could overcome these
> obstacles.

If Arizona could elect a Republican delegate to Congress and thereby show the Republican administration in Washington that Democratic domination was not certain in Arizona, the chances of statehood would increase. And a Republican delegate might get better access to the next Republican administration (which was likely to be elected given the popularity of the Roosevelt administration) than would a Democrat. The argument for Cameron resembled that made for Alexander Brodie a decade before, but it rang with more immediacy. Oklahoma (with the Indian Territory) had been admit-ted to the union the previous year. Now only Arizona and New Mexico remained outside.

The deciding factor in Arizona's 1908 congressional election was probably not Cameron's campaigning, though he did aggressively canvas the territory. The argument made by the Republicans that a Republican delegate could best facilitate statehood might not have helped much either under normal conditions. Strangely, Marcus Smith apparently gave the election to the Republicans. On October 17 he made the shocking announcement that he would be leaving the territory immediately to work for the presidential campaign of William Jennings Bryan and would not return to Arizona until after the election. Ralph Cameron thus became the first Republican elected to represent Arizona in the United States Congress since Buckey O'Neill split the vote with his Populist campaign in 1884, twenty-four years earlier. Shortly after the election lame duck President Roosevelt boosted the hopes of Arizona

Republicans by calling for the immediate admission of New Mexico and Arizona as separate states in his final address to Congress on December 8, 1908.

With a Republican congressional delegate, Cameron, a more traditional Republican president, Taft, and a Republican organization strengthened by the energetic leadership of Chairman Hovel Smith in the 1908 campaign, the prospects and mood of Arizona Republicans improved greatly. Hovel Smith and Ralph Cameron soon set about the next phase of party building in Arizona—allocation of patronage.[51]

Traditionally presidential appointments were deferred to the senator or senators from that state who were members of the president's own party. In the territories, the congressional representative was given the honor of naming appointees. Roosevelt was unaffected by this tradition in Arizona because Arizona could not, during his presidency, elect a Republican congressional delegate. He had also proven in 1904 that he could ignore the advice and wishes of the party machine in Arizona and still expect backing. He slighted the party machine in the other territories in the same fashion. Roosevelt's attitude toward his own party in the territories contrasts sharply with the traditional deference which he did show in the big states. In Texas, for example, which was also heavily Democratic, but with a much larger population and correspondingly larger party machine which he could not manipulate easily, Roosevelt had instructed applicants to be sure to get party endorsement first. Mainstream Arizona Republicans were naturally upset by Roosevelt's apparent lack of concern for their advancement as he routinely passed them over for his Rough Riders, who

---

51 Among the job applicants who were given serious consideration but not chosen are two familiar names. Isaac Stoddard, who had been discredited as territorial secretary in his battle with Governor Brodie over control of incorporation fees, wanted to be governor. Richard Stanton, the combative Ranger and former Rough Rider, wanted to take Daniels' place as US Marshal.

generally were not active Republicans, and often were, in fact or heart, Democrats.

The most visible of the "Roosevelt Republicans" were the most vulnerable targets in the Arizona Republican purge which began in 1909. Marshal Daniels, US Attorney Alexander, and Tombstone District Court Clerk George Wilcox had all been Democrats prior to their association with Roosevelt. Alexander and Wilcox made a fight for their jobs, as did Governor Kibbey. The intent of the Republican machine is clear in a letter from territorial committeeman J. C. Adams to Ralph Cameron dated February 4, 1909. In this letter Adams recommended considerable change in order to secure Republican power, and also warned that "Kibbey and his outfit of office holders will try to show you as little consideration as they have shown the party and organization in the past."

Marshal Daniels, who was among the most loyal of Roosevelt's followers in Arizona at that time, found that loyalty to be a decided disadvantage now. During the joint statehood debate, Daniels had boldly and firmly declared himself in favor of joint statehood. This made him a liability to the Republican Party in 1909. Some party leaders did not want Daniels holding office when elections to the impending constitutional convention occurred, because he would be a reminder to the voters that the Republicans had sponsored the hated joint statehood proposal. Charles Overlook, who eventually succeeded Daniels, wrote to Cameron on May 12, 1909 that "should Daniels hold his office until his term ends or be re-appointed, it would be political suicide for Arizona."

Ben Daniels was a very difficult problem for Arizona's Republican machine because Roosevelt wanted him reappointed. A memorandum from the ex-President to his friend and chosen successor, William Howard Taft, listed the names of only eleven federal appointees who, according to Roosevelt, "have been staunch adherents of Mr. Taft under stress of adverse assault in positions not of the first rank." Daniels is the only Arizonan named on that list. Hovel Smith was especially interested in rewarding the party supporters and punishing those who did not support the party in the 1908 election. Mindful of the support Daniels received from Roosevelt, Smith urged Cameron to press for Daniels' removal saying:

> I have heard rumors to the effect that President Roosevelt had requested President Taft to reappoint Mr. Ben Daniels US Marshal. Mr. Daniels will undoubtedly fulfill the duties of the office in a creditable manner, but the fact is he is a Democrat, did not take any interest in the campaign last Fall and did not contribute any amount of money which should be forthcoming from him, and I do not feel he is entitled to consideration at the hands of the Republican Party at all.

President Taft complied with the wishes of Arizona Republicans without completely ignoring those of the former president. He reassigned Ben Daniels as an Indian agent in Wisconsin. The Republican machine must have been delighted. Not only was Ben Daniels out of the marshal's office, but he was also a thousand miles away. The job did not work out for Daniels though. Unhappy in the position, he resigned within six months and returned to Arizona.

J. L. B. Alexander had no better claim to Republican Party membership than did Ben Daniels. He had campaigned to secure the Arizona delegation to the 1908 Republican convention for Taft, which alienated him from the party regulars. Machine Republicans resented Roosevelt for passing them over for appointments throughout his presidency. They would protest by trying to send an uninstructed delegation to the party convention, rather than one instructed for

Roosevelt's man, Taft. Alexander, in his support of Taft, was representing the interests of his patron against the Arizona party machine. After Taft's nomination, Alexander disengaged from politicking during the 1908 general election campaign thus showing no support for fellow Republicans in Arizona. Consequently, he earned the wrath of the Republican Central Committee. Alexander was apparently unaware at first that his job was in jeopardy. In an anxious telegram to the attorney general he stated:

> On my arrival here tenth instant to attend session United States court my attention was called to an article appear-ing in a Democratic newspaper of this place which stated that Charges [sic] against my personal character and con-duct had been forward to Washington to prevent my reappointment as United States Attorney for Arizona. If such Charges [sic] have been filed with you against me they are without foundation and false and have been made or inspired by parties whom I have had occasion to deal with in my official capacity for infractions of the federal statutes.

The US attorney discovered later that the only charges leveled against him were that he was not a good Republican, and he should make way for an organization man. The Republican Central Committee of Arizona sent two telegrams and some individual letters to the President protesting his reappointment without stating any reason for the protest or any charges against Alexander. One letter sent to President Taft clearly states the situation. The author wrote:

> I understand the appointment of Attorney General [sic] for this Territory will soon take place and there being some newspaper talk of the reappointment of

Mr. J.B. [sic] Alexander thought I would interest myself sufficiently to let you know from what I can learn that the same would cause considerable dissension in the Republican party. The majority of Republicans have been looking forward to the appointment of Mr. J.E. Morrison to that office and which I know would give entire satisfaction as he was one of the principal supporters of Hon. Ralph Cameron during his campaign and materially assisted him in his being elected….

The author, Ben Frankenberg, apparently knew what he was writing about. Alexander's successor was J.E. Morrison.

US Attorney Alexander gathered recommendations of many prominent Arizonans despite the opposition of the territories party leaders. The chief justice and two associate justices of the Arizona Supreme Court, the governor, and most of the recent ex-governors of the territory, and editors of leading Republican newspapers supported him. However, he secured only one recommendation from an official party source. He had no real chance of reappointment, and he was angry about his removal.

Alexander was not alone in his anger. The 1910 dismissal of George Wilcox came at the hands of a friend and ally, and it made him very bitter. Wilcox had held the position of clerk of the Tombstone court for about eight years. The position happened to be one of the best paying jobs in the territory and Wilcox was one of Roosevelt's favorites.[52] When charges were filed against Judge Fletcher M. Doan of that court four years earlier, Wilcox went to Washington to speak with the President and was influential in getting those charges dropped. Ironically, Wilcox held his position at the pleasure of the judge, and President Taft threatened the judge with his

---

52 As mentioned earlier, Roosevelt even briefly considered appointing Wilcox as Arizona governor.

own dismissal if he did not dismiss Wilcox. Doan complied with the President's demand. Wilcox then declared that he would file charges against Doan for previously undisclosed wrongdoing. He also "declared war on the Republican leaders." The Justice Department investigated the charges Wilcox made and declared them "Malicious and without 'foundation.'" In time Wilcox, Alexander, and Daniels would change parties again and challenge the Republicans who had rebuked them.

In the summer of 1910, just as the Republican machine completed its purge of the renegade Roosevelt element, one of Roosevelt's most ardent and formidable Rough Rider supporters entered the Arizona political mix. This was John C. Greenway, the new manager of the Calumet and Arizona Copper Company in Warren, a twin city of Bisbee, Arizona. Though Greenway was a southerner, he came to Arizona from Minnesota where, as a mine executive, he had designed the comfortable, well-planned company town of Coleraine. He was a man of great talent and energy. At Yale University he had excelled in football and baseball, was elected class president, and was voted most popular man on campus. As a Rough Rider lieutenant, Greenway won Roosevelt's praise for his remarkable "energy, eagerness to duty, and great physical strength" and as a man "who could be counted upon with absolute certainly, not only in every emergency, but in all routine work."

Greenway and Roosevelt had remained close friends since the war, corresponding frequently and getting together at times. Greenway was a guest at the White House on several occasions and, as has been mentioned, he accompanied Roosevelt on his 1905 tour of the South. Roosevelt even offered Greenway a position in his administration as Commissioner of the General Land Office, asking not because Greenway needed a job, but as a favor to the President. The impact of Jack Greenway on Arizona politics would not be noticeable until 1912, though his presence in the territory probably delighted his Rough

Rider colleagues, a dozen of whom lived in the Bisbee vicinity, including Postmaster George J. McCabe, former Populist, now a Roosevelt Republican.

The big news that summer for Roosevelt supporters was the return of the ex-president from his hunting adventure in Africa and his subsequent tour of Europe. The return of the popular Roosevelt to the United States after an absence of more than a year was a celebrated event for the whole country. The former president's motorcade through New York City attracted the largest crowd ever assembled for any event in the history of the city up to that time. Roosevelt's manner on returning to America was more confident than ever. Archie Butt, long time military aide to the Roosevelt administration, described the Roosevelt he met that day as "bigger, broader, capable of greater good or greater evil...."

The Rough Riders who met their colonel that day were also impressive according to the *Arizona Republican,* though they were little mentioned by the *New York Times.* Heralded by the Arizona newspaper as "Second only in interest to the returning traveler," a large number of splendidly clad Rough Riders were among the five thousand Spanish War veterans who marched in the parade. The *Republican* reported of its native sons:

> The troops wore yellow khaki with buckskin leggings and broad brimmed gray slouch hats. Their horses were accountred [sic] with heavy military saddles, as though ready for campaign.

They moved in battalion form, their ranks extended for two blocks, with flags flying and their Rough Rider band playing.

The most prominent southwesterners among them included Thomas Rynning, former Ranger Captain and now prison superintendent, George Wilcox, the former clerk of the Tombstone court, James C. Goodwin, politician and sometimes member of the Arizona House of Representatives, and Will McGinty, who had been one of the best horsemen in the regiment.[53] Others from the region also included C. B. Ivy, A. R. Russell, and E. W. Waterbury.

Two days before Roosevelt stepped on to American soil at New York harbor, the United States Senate finally passed the Enabling Act for Arizona statehood. Twice before the House had passed an enabling act for Arizona only to have it killed in the Senate. This 1910 act, which had been passed in the House back in January, did not come up for a vote in the Senate until June 16. Unlike previous statehood efforts, this act had the full support of both the President and the ex-president, and the Republican national platform of 1908 had promised statehood for New Mexico and Arizona. The Senate vote was 64 to zero with 27 abstentions. Senator Beveridge was instrumental in constructing the Senate version of the bill and bringing it to the floor before the summer recess. The House quickly affirmed the Senate version, thus avoiding the need for a conference committee. With the passage of the Enabling Act, Senator Beveridge sent a congratulatory letter to the people of Arizona in which he said, "I have labored for Arizona's people instead of for those who sought to exploit them." Acknowledging the conflict over the joint statehood proposal, he said, "I like a good and clean fighter and I have never seen cleaner or better fighters than you have proved to be."

When Arizona elected members to the Constitutional Convention of 1910, the territory's Republicans were disappointed. Forty-one Democrats and only eight Republicans were elected to the convention. With this disparity in representation between the parties, Republicans were naturally concerned that the constitution written by

---

53   In *Rough Riders* Roosevelt tells of how McGinty was notorious for being unable to keep in step while marching. He also said that McGinty "never walked a hundred yards if by any possibility he could ride."

the largely Democratic convention would be more populist and socialist than the Republican control Congress or the Taft administration could accept. If the Arizona constitution were rejected by the US Congress or the President, Arizona statehood would be set back again, and Arizona Republicans would feel the backlash. This would be a major blow to the struggling Republican Party in Arizona.

Arizona historian Marshall Trimble makes the interesting observation that, to him, the constitution written at that convention was not socialist, nor even really liberal in general, but rather "traditional and even a little old fashioned." Trimble explains that years of conflict between appointed Republican governors and Democratic legislatures had influenced the Democratic convention delegates to make the office of governor weak while the national trend was to strengthen executive power so that government could run more efficiently. Richard Sloan, Arizona's last territorial governor concurs with Trimble's assessment, calling the Arizona Constitution "In some ways…decidedly reactionary." In other ways it was progressive.

Probably the most popular reforms in government at that time, initiative, referendum, and recall, promoted participatory government. In October 1909, before the Arizona Constitutional Convention began its work, President Taft came to Phoenix and expressed his dislike for these new forms of progressive democracy. He also reminded Arizonans that the US Congress would have to approve the new Arizona constitution and he would have to sign it. The warning went unheeded by the Democratic majority. When the constitution was completed it included initiative, referendum, and recall of all elected officials, including judges. All but one of the Republicans at the convention refused to sign it.

Arizona's struggle for statehood figured in the national battle between Taft and Roosevelt that had been developing almost since the day of President Taft's election.[54] By 1911, Roosevelt, perhaps the most loved and admired man in the country, vigorously criticized his handpicked successor. In March, the American icon, Roosevelt, came to Arizona for the dedication of Roosevelt Dam which had been funded by the National Irrigation Act of 1902. Speaking to a crowd in Phoenix, the ex-president briefly criticized the administration for opposing the will of the Arizona People. Taft had threatened to veto the Arizona Constitution because of his opposition to the provision of recall of the judiciary. Roosevelt frankly admitted that he too did not favor the recall of judges, but he also asserted that Arizonans had the right to decide the issue for themselves.

The colonel made no further attacks on the Taft administration during his visit. He instead enjoyed several days of positive communion with Arizona and its people. He spoke warmly about the Rough Riders saying "…no body of men can ever have quite the claim upon me that these have with whom I marched, in whose company I fought, who lay in the trenches with me, and shared all around on fair terms on hard-tack when that was all there was to go around, and it was mighty good at times." At the Arizona capitol, the *Republican* reported that the colonel "looked longingly and lovingly at the battle scarred and bullet torn emblem" which was the flag of the Arizona troops, now enshrined in glass. "I can almost see Wright carrying it," he said. A Rough Rider luncheon in Phoenix was closed to the public and the *Republican* reported only that the room was carefully decorated with Arizona

---

54 Historian Nathan Miller says that the first event in the Roosevelt-Taft rift occurred when Roosevelt took offense to Taft's thank you letter shortly after his election in which the President-elect said that Roosevelt was one of the two men who had contributed most to his election, the other being Taft's brother. Roosevelt felt that his contribution was paramount to Taft's election and later compared this statement to saying that "Abraham Lincoln and the bond seller Jay Cooke saved the Union."

poppies and Indian blankets, and a large number of Rough Riders attended. [55]

After the luncheon, a warm encounter between Roosevelt and Tom Rynning's two young daughters caught the attention of a reporter from the *Republican*. At the conclusion of the dedication of the dam named in his honor, Roosevelt told a reporter that "with the single exception of the Grand Canyon the view of the mountains near the Roosevelt dam is the greatest and most impressive sight he has ever seen." The ex-President had brought some of his family with him. When their train was about to leave, Captain Alexander presented them with presents from the Rough Riders. Thus the romance between Roosevelt and Arizona had been reaffirmed at least for the major population center of Maricopa County.

The feeling toward Roosevelt in other parts of southern Arizona was more in doubt. Much to the disappointment of John Greenway, Roosevelt's tour did not include the boomtown of Bisbee, which was at that time, one of the largest cities in Arizona due to the success of the copper industry. Greenway thought that if Roosevelt were to make a run for the presidency in 1912, Bisbee could be important to winning Arizona. The colonel's support appeared to be weak in Bisbee and Cochise County based on Greenway's informal observations.

Though the formidable Roosevelt was considering opposing Taft in 1912, the President did not shrink from

---

55 The following Rough Riders were at that banquet:
J. L. B. Alexander of Phoenix, H.E. Berner of Tombstone, P. F. Byrne of Florence, J. D. Carter of Phoenix, C. P. Cronin now of Phoenix,   Ben Daniels of Tucson, W. A. Davidson of Ray, J. C. Goodwin of Tempe, Sam Greenwald of Florence, J. M. Hall of Phoenix, Fenn Hildreth of Phoenix, Wesley Hill of Tempe, William H. Hogie of Mesa, J. R. Kean of Glendale, G. J. McCabe of Hereford, James McClintock of Phoenix, J. H. Maxey of Yuma, Thomas Mooney of Florence, J. O. Mullen of Tempe, S. H. Rhodes of Phoenix, Henry Sells of Phoenix, P. J. Sullivan of Yuma, Charles Utting of Yuma, N. A. Vyne of Prescott, Harry White of Alhambra, P. E. Woodson of Phoenix, T. W. Pemberton of Roosevelt, Tom Rynning of Florence, Richard Stanton of Yuma, George Truman of Florence, Frank Van Siclin of Florence. H. M. Warren of Phoenix, George Wilcox now of Phoenix.

what he perceived as his duty relative to Arizona just to avoid providing Roosevelt with a campaign issue. On August 15, 1911, President Taft vetoed the Arizona statehood bill based on his disapproval of the provision in the constitution which allowed for the recall of judges.

The President's feelings were strong on the issue. His own background was more as a jurist than as a politician, and he could not bring himself to sanction the possible corruption of judicial officials by political considerations. The President, however, still favored statehood for both New Mexico and Arizona. Congress presented him with an acceptable statehood bill a week later. That bill provided that statehood would be granted to Arizona once the people had voted to remove judicial recall from the state constitution. The stipulation was not looked upon as a major stumbling block in Arizona. The territory's newspapers proclaimed that statehood had been won at last and celebrations were held throughout the territory.

Roosevelt had earlier suggested that the recall provision be left out of the constitution until after the approval of statehood. Recall could then be reinserted if the people wished. President Taft's only objection was to the recall provision, so Roosevelt's suggestion made practical sense. One of the big proponents of this alternative had been George Wilcox, now a pharmacist in Phoenix. In July 1911, as Taft's veto seemed eminent, Wilcox surveyed the area of his downtown business and reported to Ralph Cameron that 88% of voters favored elimination of recall of the judiciary if necessary, for statehood. Wilcox also had hoped that the change could be made by the convention, he cautioned that "I believe there are enough transient voters and constitutional cranks in Arizona to defeat statehood under the provision of the Nelson resolution [popular vote]." Wilcox's fear about a direct plebiscite was unwarranted. With the prize of statehood assured for a small, and by no means necessarily permanent, change in the constitution, the people voted to comply with the President's wishes. Judicial recall was voted out by a wide margin, and President Taft signed the Arizona statehood proclamation on February 14, 1912, officially creating the "Valentine State."

John Greenway was heavily influenced by Roosevelt and seems always to have agreed with him on every issue. The two saw Arizona statehood and the recall controversy as only a campaign issue against President Taft. The more substantive issue in Arizona, which greatly concerned both men, was the spill over of the Mexican Revolution. Several Mexican towns just south of the border have nearly adjacent twins in Arizona. When fighting in Augua Prieta, Sonora, sent stray bullets into the streets of Douglas, Arizona, Greenway pressured Arizona Governor Sloan to write to President Taft seeking protection for Americans in the border towns. Taft's response, Greenway reported to Roosevelt, was to advise Arizonans to "keep out of the way of Mexican bullets." Greenway was angered at the apparent apathy of the President to this threat to the security of Americans on American soil. Roosevelt's response to Greenway included these words: "I am absolutely unable to understand what the administration means by permitting the killing of Americans on American soil to go on." If he were president, Roosevelt continued, he would station troops on the border and would take possession of any town "from which shots had been fired that killed Americans."

By early 1912, machinery was being established in Arizona, as well as other states to promote the Republican nomination of Roosevelt for president. On January 26, two influential Arizonans, Dwight Heard, a Phoenix land developer, and former governor Kibbey announced the formation of the Theodore Roosevelt club of Phoenix. The next day J. L. B. Alexander, former US Attorney, wrote to Roosevelt to encourage the colonel to announce his intention to seek the nomination, telling Roosevelt that clubs such as the one in Phoenix were forming all over Arizona. A few months later Alexander wrote to Robert Patterson, who had served directly under him as a first lieutenant, asking for the names of Republicans in Graham County who favored Roosevelt. John Greenway led the Cochise County Roosevelt club in Bisbee and Douglas. Ben Daniels organized the Pima County club. A "Roosevelt to Win" rally was held in Phoenix on February 5.

Many other Rough Riders also campaigned for the colonel in other states. At the national level, Rough Rider Frank Knox was the vice chairman of the Roosevelt committee. He had been Republican state chairman in Michigan. Congressman George Curry of New Mexico lent his energy and prestige to the Roosevelt campaign in that state where he had once been an ardent Democrat before Roosevelt appointed him governor. David Goodrich and Rock Channing were involved in the New York campaign.

The problem faced by the Roosevelt forces in Arizona was the same as that encountered by the colonel's forces in other states without primary elections. Presidential control of patronage placed the party machine at the disposal of the President, regardless of the feelings of the rank and file. This was especially true in states like Arizona where the President's party was in the minority and a large percentage of the machine politicians depended on the President for their jobs. Not surprisingly, the Executive Committee of the Arizona Republican Party endorsed President Taft "without reservation." But if the nomination process could be changed to a direct primary election, Roosevelt backers felt that the Arizona delegation would be pledged to Roosevelt.

The other big problem Roosevelt supporters faced was Roosevelt himself. The exploratory, indefinite campaign, which the ex-president was running at the time, cost him support. Few mainstream Republicans would risk their political careers by siding with Roosevelt without being certain of his candidacy. Roosevelt finally did announce in late February. The announcement may have been reluctant since Roosevelt had little realistic chance of wrenching the nomination from an incumbent president, but he had gone too far in his criticism. He had started a movement which he could neither stop nor abandon. At one point in 1911, Roosevelt had expressed to a gathering of state Republican chairmen that he did not want to run because the race might destroy his reputation, to which Michigan Chairman and Rough Rider Knox retorted, "Colonel, I never knew you to show the white feather, and you should not do so now."

Roosevelt's Arizona supporters experienced difficulties which, though they may not have been typical of the entire country, were not unusual. No direct primary law was instituted in Arizona, so the allocation of Arizona's delegates was left to convention. Cochise County Republicans were so split that two different county conventions were held. John Greenway was chosen to lead the Cochise Roosevelt delegation to the state convention. Roosevelt telegraphed his congratulations to Greenway the day before the opening of the convention and added, "If our men are unseated I hope they will hold a separate convention." When, in fact, many of the Roosevelt delegates were being unseated at the Tucson convention, the entire Roosevelt delegation moved to the back of the room, held their own convention, and elected delegates to the national convention among whom were Greenway and Daniels.

In the states which had primary elections, Roosevelt did very well, but this meant little in securing the nomination in 1912. The ex-president won nine of twelve primaries, including Taft's home state of Ohio. Robert LaFollette won two. President Taft won only one primary election. Roosevelt had won by large majorities in most of these states, proving that he was the choice of the people, but he remained realistic about his chances, saying, "My belief is that I shall probably

—

not be nominated at Chicago. But they will have to steal the delegates outright in order to prevent my nomination, and if the stealing is flagrant no one can tell what the result will be." At this point Roosevelt seems to have had a plan for just this contingency.

Arizona Delegate Ben Daniels appears to have been politically naïve, but, perhaps, he was very crafty and was using inside information. He bet five hundred dollars that Roosevelt would be nominated in Chicago. Marshal Daniels and his associates from Arizona, Greenway, Heard, et.al., were among the many Roosevelt delegates refused seats. Taft of course was nominated, and the Roosevelt backers held a separate meeting which became the inception of the Progressive Party. Greenway, Knox, and one other Rough Rider, Frank Frantz, former Oklahoma governor, had the distinction to serve on the committee which informed Roosevelt that he had been nominated for the presidency by an independent party. Ben Daniels now claimed to have won his bet.[56]

Greenway returned to Arizona furious. He wrote to fellow Rough Rider Alexander, "I am through with the GOP." His reason being "the stealing of a nomination for the presidency." Greenway, Alexander, Dwight Heard, and others now formed the Progressive Party of Arizona. "Governor Kibbey is reluctant to quit the Republican Party," Greenway's letter to Alexander continued, "but it is up to you to persuade him and Judge Kent." Preparations for another convention moved ahead rapidly.

The organizational meeting of the Arizona Progressive Party was held in Phoenix on July 30. The key figures at that meeting were of course Heard and Greenway who would be joined by E. L. Cummings, Thomas Marshall, and J. F.

---

56 Both parties to the bet had each deposited their $500 with a bank. The winner was to collect the $1000. Eventually the money held by the bank was returned to each man. Contracts involving gambling were unenforceable. Gambling had been illegal in Arizona since 1907.

Cleveland as delegates to the National Progressive Convention to be held in Chicago.

J. L. B. Alexander was named campaign chairman. Arizona's Rough Riders and their many allies rallied around the colonel for another fight. Besides Greenway, Alexander, and Daniels, other Arizona Rough Riders who became active Progressive Party workers included George Wilcox, Richard Stanton, and Charles Utting.

When the time came for the national convention, Arizona's delegation was set at thirteen, including one woman.[57] The only Rough Rider to make that second trip to Chicago in 1912 was Ben Daniels. John Greenway was unable to get away from his duties at the Warren mine. Greenway also experienced another disappointment a month later when Roosevelt's campaign tour came through Arizona, but no provision was made for an appearance in Bisbee-Warren.

Roosevelt gave a lengthy major policy address in Phoenix. After an aide finally interrupted, reminding him of the time, the colonel exclaimed, "Great heavens! Have I talked an hour and a quarter?" He had focused on President Taft's insistence on the removal of the recall provision from the Arizona Constitution as a violation of the right of the people to self-rule. Roosevelt's words that day were remarkably consistent with the assertions he had made regarding the recall during his visit the previous year. He still maintained that he would, as a public official, feel duty bound to advise against recall, but he would accept the decision since the people's right to rule was the focus of the Progressive Party. In that Phoenix speech, Roosevelt defined the people's right to rule and the duty of public officials in this way: "It doesn't mean that I am only to advise the people to do what I think they want to have me advise them to do, not a bit. If I am fit to be a public servant at

---

57 The lone female in the delegation was Mrs. Frank Townsend. At their inception the Progressives declared their commitment to equal suffrage for women.

all, I will honestly advise what I think ought to be advised, but this is advice, it is not dictatorship, and if they don't choose to take it, all right. But it goes. And that is what I feel the attitude of the public servant should be...."

Roosevelt had little real chance in the election and, therefore, had nothing to lose by establishing a high level of politics; he might even find in a losing campaign a greater place in history. But in any case, Roosevelt and the Progressives appeared to be raising the level of politics in America. Politicians were challenged to be statesmen, and statesmen were challenged to be true public servants, policy advisors, not policy makers.

The Arizona Progressives got a morale boost in early October when Dwight Heard arranged for the purchase of the *Arizona Republican*. A corporation was formed with ten stockholders. Dwight and Maie Heard held 360 of the 1,000 shares; most of the remainder were held by three people in Chicago; John Greenway was also a stockholder with 27 shares. Heard was the corporation president and chief editor. Throughout the first month of the new ownership, Heard published his personal statement about why the paper was purchased and what he hoped to accomplish with the paper. During that time he also published the platform of the Progressive Party daily and covered Roosevelt's campaign extensively.

Despite the enthusiastic efforts of the Progressives in Arizona and Roosevelt's personal appeal, they were probably doomed from the start because they were, after all, an off shoot of a minority party in the state. Considering this, Roosevelt did remarkably well in Arizona, matching (even slightly exceeding) his popular percentage in the nation overall. This was no small accomplishment because Socialist candidate Eugene Debs polled much higher in Arizona than he did nationwide. He actually out polled the incumbent president in the "baby state." Greenway telegraphed Roosevelt his congratulations on a hard-fought campaign and mentioned a small personal victory; Bisbee-Warren had voted for Roosevelt. Progressives could take consolation in that a progressive Democrat had been elected and a new party had been forged which offered hope for the future. The table below gives the percentage of the popular vote for each candidate in Arizona and the nation as well as the electoral vote.

	Arizona	*US*	*Electoral Vote*
Wilson	44.0%	42.5%	435
Roosevelt	29.6	27.9	88
Taft	12.8	23.6	8
Debs	13.6	6.0	0

The Progressive Party had an unmistakable evangelical quality to it from the moment that the Roosevelt delegates bolted the Republican convention with the chant "Thou shalt not steal." The popular hymn "Onward Christian Soldiers" became the party anthem and was sung often at the national convention. Senator Beveridge gave the keynote address at the first party convention, and excited the crusading spirit with his words, "not reluctantly, then, but eagerly, not with faint hearts, but strong, do we now advance upon the enemies of the people." Roosevelt, himself, had told his supporters, "We stand at Armageddon and we battle for the Lord." This curious mixture of politics and religion made certain that the Progressive Party would live beyond the 1912 election. Those who found this new religion meaningful could not easily caste it aside.

The religiosity of the movement also created unique problems for the fledgling party. Religious truth is timeless, but in the haste within which this religion was established much doctrine was left unsettled. Theodore Roosevelt, the prophet, was a whirlwind mass of energy and contradiction. He would soon find himself in conflict with many members of his flock. Commitment to the party would be tested in the adversity of the next four years.

CHAPTER 7

Death of the Heroic Era, 1913–1919

*Death was the black horse that came some day into
every man's camp, and no matter when that day came
a brave man should be booted and spurred and ready
to ride him out.*

—*William "Buckey" O'Neill*
Captain, A Troop
Roosevelt's Rough Riders[58]

After the 1912 election, the Progressive Party declined rapidly. The party was in some ways the victim of the times as global problems dwarfed its domestic agenda, but inability to expand its political base also contributed to its demise. In these changing times, the Rough Rider heroes of '98, too, found that they had become irrelevant and their war archaic even before the twentieth anniversary of the famous

---

58 This is from a short story which O'Neill had written. This is often quoted and was, in fact, used by Dale Walker in the title of his O'Neill biography. The quote is also contained in Paul Andrew Hutton, "T.R. Takes Charge," *American History*, vol. 33, no. 3, (August 1998): 36.

San Juan charge. Those who were to contribute would have to meet a new world on new terms. Roosevelt's leadership would falter too.

His showing in the 1912 election had proven that he could be a viable presidential candidate for the new party, but the party itself had not done well. Having drawn nearly all its members from among the Republicans, the Progressive Party found itself smaller and weaker than the now reduced and anemic GOP. Without a significant number of Democratic converts, followers of the Bull Moose would see their party doomed to remain the smallest and weakest of the three parties.

Inability to appeal to Democrats was a great intrinsic defect everywhere for Roosevelt's party. Having fused with the Populists in the 1890s, the Democratic Party had an outlet for reform minded members. And the Democratic president, Woodrow Wilson, who projected the image of a progressive, discouraged defection at the national level during the mid-term election campaign of 1914 by delivering major progressive legislation just in time that year—the Federal Trade Commission Act, September 26, and the Clayton Act, October 15. The latter insured the devotion of labor to the Democratic cause by including provision guaranteeing the basic rights of unions. Samuel Gompers declared it to be the "Magna Carta of Labor."

The prospects for Progressives in Arizona were even more dismal than those of Progressives elsewhere. The Arizona Progressive Party was, after all, a splinter from the minority party. In the presidential campaign of 1912 Arizona Progressives had been hampered by severely limited funds. According to state campaign chairman J. L. B. Alexander, as of October 21, total campaign contributions were only $1,329.88 of which Alexander had contributed $450 himself. Arizona's own popular Democratic governor, George W.P. Hunt, was also progressive and pro-labor though he proved to be vulnerable in 1916.[59] To expand and survive, Arizona Progressives would have to look to the Republican Party with the prospect of being reabsorbed.

The support of Dwight Heard's newspaper continued to boost Progressive hopes. Heard was a true believer in progressivism and willing to invest in its future. He was the unchallenged leader of the Arizona Progressive Party and the *Republican* was the party mouthpiece. But the next three key men at the top of the party were all former Rough Rider officers. J. L. B. Alexander was the state campaign chairman for 1912, 1914, and 1916. John Greenway was a prominent, unofficial spokesman with direct connection to Theodore Roosevelt. And George Wilcox became the party secretary.

Alexander's position as campaign chairman was probably due to the fact that he was the most politically experienced. He had been involved with politics on the Democratic side from the early 1890s until about the time of his appointment as US attorney, when he became a "Roosevelt Republican." In 1893, he was selected as part of a four-man nonpartisan committee to lobby for Arizona statehood in Washington, DC. Wilcox had some limited political experience as an elected justice of the peace in Bisbee in 1900 after losing his bid for the territorial legislature two years earlier. He, of course, had observed politics for many years after that as court clerk in Tombstone.

Greenway is the only one of this group who seems to have found politics distasteful, at that time anyway. He declined to attend the Progressive National Committee conference in Chicago the month after the 1912 election. Then the following month, in the frustration of the moment, he declared that he was through with politics. Intense personal loyalty to Roosevelt and belief in Roosevelt's ability and character, however,

---

59 Hunt lost the very close 1916 election to Republican Jack Campbell, but later regained his office on appeal to the courts. He was given the votes of Democrats who had marked a straight party ticket then voted for Campbell for governor as their only cross over vote.

prevented Greenway from walking away from Roosevelt's party just yet. Alexander and Wilcox were apparently devoted to the colonel and to the cause of progressivism. They also may have been partially motivated by other factors, as well, such as desire for revenge or to gain appointed positions again.

The Republican Party in Arizona began courtship of the Progressive Party soon after the 1912 election. As early as April 1913, Republican leader Lorenzo Hubbell proposed a joint meeting of the executive committees of both parties with the goal of unification under the name "Progressive-Republicans." John Greenway was opposed to any negotiations with the Republicans or any merger with either of the two major parties.

He proposed that Democrats, including Governor Hunt, would be welcome in the Progressive Party. He did not, however, offer suggestions as to how these Democrats might be recruited. Roosevelt insisted that the Progressive Party remain independent.

In February of the midterm election year 1914, Progressive secretary George Wilcox established a permanent party office in Phoenix. Soon after this he began writing articles about progressivism and the party for Heard's newspaper.

As the 1914 elections approached, Arizona's Progressive Party leaders struggled with how best to maximize the impact of the still new party in a way which would promote future growth.[60] Fielding a full array of candidates would give the party some legitimacy, but only if a reasonable number of those candidates could be elected. Since the party was small, the pool of possible party candidates was limited. And for those Progressive Party members who qualified, candidacy under the party banner was a dismal prospect. They could expect to be underfunded by the party while, at the same time, needing to

---

60 Progressive involvement in the 1912 campaign had been largely limited to the presidential race.

campaign harder than either of their two major opponents in order to draw the large cross over vote needed for victory.

By the end of June the party had still not decided on a course of action. Alexander favored the endorsement of a mixed ticket. His formula at the highest level was a Democrat for governor, a progressive Republican, "like Kibbey," for Senator, and a Progressive for Congress. He hoped that the Progressive leaders could influence the major parties to nominate candidates favorable to Progressives. Most Arizona Progressives appeared more comfortable among Republicans than among Democrats. In preparation for the 1914 election, men from both Progressive and Republican parties moved toward cooperation and merger at the county level despite Roosevelt's announced wishes and the official state policy non-amalgamation. Reacting to the pressure for union with Republicans and because he had more hope of success with the weaker Republican Party, Alexander reluctantly began negotiations with the GOP.

He quickly became disenchanted. By July 10, he had given up hope of working with the Republicans and was insisting that his Progressives produce a full ticket at the state level and encouraging the county organizations to do the same. He chose to run for attorney general and began scrambling to fill the state ticket. To Greenway, he hinted that someone from Cochise County might be a strong candidate for Corporation Commission.[61] Party Secretary Wilcox accepted the nomination for sheriff of Maricopa County (Phoenix). The Democratic Party swept all state offices that year, having benefited greatly from the split between the Progressives and the Republicans.

The Progressive Party was fading away. The war in Europe, problems on the Mexican border, and the possibility of war

---

61 Many of the most productive copper mines were in Cochise County, and copper mining was the dominant industry in Arizona.

with Mexico diverted the attention of many Americans from domestic politics. The Mexican Revolution, which began in 1910, spilled over along the US-Mexican border. As early as March 1911, Roosevelt had written to Taft offering to raise an entire division of Rough Riders for service in the event of war with Mexico. The ex-president had apparently given the formation of this division some serious thought. Though he knew that "there is…one chance in a thousand of serious trouble," he had developed a list of potential officers down to company commanders. At least three of his original regiment would be regimental commanders; these were John Greenway, John McIlhenny, and Gordon Johnston. McIlhenny and Greenway were civilians, while Johnston was a career army officer.

Less than a month after Roosevelt had written this letter, the battle in Augua Prieta, Sonora, referred to in the previous chapter, was fought. The streets of Douglas cleared while residents watched the battle from the relative safety of their roofs. Shortly after this, another border battle at Juarez sent bullets into El Paso, Texas. Four Americans were reported to have been killed on that occasion. Roosevelt believed that Taft's response was wholly inadequate.

The Taft administration preferred diplomacy to war and the crisis abated temporarily but reappeared in 1914 during Wilson's first term. In a siege at Naco, Sonora, the soldiers of Venustiano Carranza backed up against the border. To protect themselves, the citizens of Naco, Arizona, to the immediate north, piled sandbags along the border. From that time on, the revolution could not be fully contained within the northern border of Mexico. Within two months of the beginning of the Naco siege, over fifty Americans along the border had been wounded, mostly by stray bullets. Feeling increased pressure to act and hoping to topple the government of Victorio Huerta, President Wilson reacted to a small incident at Tampico on the east coast of Mexico by sending in marines to occupy Vera Cruz. Greenway wrote to Roosevelt in May saying, "We must take Mexico."

The border problems continued. In March 1916, Francisco "Pancho" Villa made his raid on Columbus, New Mexico, killing seventeen Americans. President Wilson called up nearly 200,000 National Guardsmen to patrol the border in 1916 and sent General John J. Pershing into Mexico to try to capture Villa. Roosevelt thought the way that the National Guard was used was "wicked," providing "most of the hardship of war, without the benefits of efficient war," but the ex-president no longer expected to lead troops into Mexico. After the sinking of the *Lusitania* in 1915, Roosevelt planned to lead his division to the western front. Two weeks after the *Lusitania* disaster, he wrote to his son, Archie, "Probably, as you suggested, in the event of war, I would send you out at once under Jack Greenway."

The Progressive Party of Arizona, like those of most other states, did not attempt to field candidates for the 1916 election. Ben Daniels ran for Pima County sheriff on the Republican ticket and asked for the support of his Progressive friends. The Progressive Party planned its national convention to coincide with that of the Republican Party in Chicago. Progressives hoped to influence the Republicans to nominate Roosevelt, their one clear first choice. Greenway cautioned Roosevelt to accept the nomination of both parties or none at all.

While Roosevelt probably initially hesitated to run for president again after the 1912 campaign, by 1916 he apparently wanted to be president again. Paradoxically, Roosevelt renewed his interest in the presidency because of his desire to change the direction of American foreign policy, and he realized that the majority of the American people did not support his foreign policy ideas. He also speculated that if the mood of the country was fundamentally opposed to heroic action he would be ineffective as president. He wrote to his confidant, Henry Cabot Lodge, in February 1916, a letter which illustrates some of the frustration of this man of heroic action in a suddenly more complex, non-heroic world:

> ...it is utterly idle to nominate me if the country is in a mood either for timidity or of that base and complacent materialism which find expression in the phrase "Safety first." If the country is not determined to put honor and duty ahead of safety, then the people most emphatically do not wish me for President and the party cannot afford to run me for President; for I will not take back my one finger's breadth anything I have said during the last eighteen months about national and international duty or apologize for anything I did while I was President. Unless the country is somewhere near a mood of at least half-heroism it will be utterly useless to nominate me. I do not, as a matter of fact, think that there would have been war if I had been President but if, in order to stop the murder of American women and children on the high seas or in Mexico it had been necessary to go to war, I would have gone to war, <in thirty minutes> and if taking the action I would have taken, as outlined in my speech last Sunday, on behalf of Belgium when Germany invaded Belgium had brought war, I would have accepted war rather than refuse to act as in my judgment the national honor demanded.

Despite Roosevelt's misgivings, bitter contempt for President Wilson drove him toward another campaign. "I am so red-hot against Wilson and Bryan [Secretary of State William Jennings Bryan] that it is difficult for me to contain myself," the colonel wrote in December 1914. Roosevelt's antagonism with Wilson involved unhappiness with the President's slow plodding on domestic issues, true disgust with his foreign policies, and a perception that he had usurped and corrupted the concept of "progressivism." The bull moose and the college professor were bound to conflict on their approach to progressivism.

While Roosevelt would have plunged ahead at full speed, Wilson moved cautiously and questioned the constitutionality of some progressive proposals. Roosevelt wrote with venom in one typical letter:

> ...he [Wilson] does not represent the Progressive ideal at all. I do not think we have had a more reactionary President than Wilson, in every sense of the word "reactionary." Moreover, I think he is entirely insincere; and he and Bryan...have in all international matters put this country lower than it has ever been for a century. I think Wilson and the Subhumans.... As regards Mexico and the European War, he has been beneath contempt.

Domestic policy, rather than foreign policy, was the more popular topic at the Progressive convention of 1916. Progressives needed reconciliation, not controversy, to have any voice in national affairs. Republicans also wanted reconciliation. Each party appointed a committee to confer with the other on a joint nominee. The Republicans were somewhat flexible in their position, saying "anyone...but Roosevelt." They eventually nominated Charles Evans Hughes who was progressive enough to reunite the party.

On August 25, 1916, in his last official act as state campaign chairman, J. L. B. Alexander sent a telegram to Judge Hughes pledging the support of the Progressives of Arizona. The next day Alexander submitted his resignation from the chairmanship, citing the inability of the state party to field candidates "due to lack of interest." He had decided at that time to join the Republican Party, which he believed then "has always stood and now stands for nationalism and progress." He had made a complete conversion. He derided the Democratic Party, of which he had been a member for many years, saying that it "has stood and now stands for sectionalism and non-advancement." George Wilcox also quickly rejoined the GOP, disregarding his Democratic roots. He soon claimed to be "an active republican [sic], deeply interested in the success and welfare of his party and even taking a helpful part in promoting its growth and insuring its success." Greenway was a nominal Republican, and the party chose him as a presidential elector, probably as a gesture of reconciliation to the Progressives.

The complete reunification of the Republican Party was sealed by Roosevelt's support for Hughes. Roosevelt, of course, deplored Wilson, especially because of what Roosevelt perceived as the timid approach which Wilson took in foreign affairs. Roosevelt may also have seen a personal payoff should Hughes win. On the opening day of the two conventions that summer, Greenway had written to Roosevelt suggesting that their chances of bringing about Roosevelt's dream of a rough rider division in the European War would be much improved under Hughes. On June 26, after the conventions had finished and the Progressives were still trying to decide on a course, Roosevelt asked the Progressive National Committee to support Hughes and the majority voted to comply with his wish.

The next day Roosevelt instructed Greenway to proceed with raising troops. Greenway and Johnston were to be appointed colonels in command of regiments. David Goodrich was to be designated either a lieutenant colonel or a major. At least two other Rough Riders were included among Roosevelt's choices for his officers. They were William E. Dame of New Mexico and Rock Channing of New York. Alexander Brodie who had retired from the army in 1913 for having reached the age limit of sixty-four also offered his services. At the time that war was declared in April 1917, Roosevelt pleaded for the creation of the division with both President Wilson and Secretary of War Newton Baker. In refusing Roosevelt's offer, President Wilson said that it would be "dramatic" action in a situation which called for "practical and scientific" procedure. Roosevelt quickly notified the men he had recruited so that those who still wished to serve could make their individual applications. Greenway planned to go to war, but in the meantime, he continued to run the mine in Warren.

That summer the International Workers of the World (IWW) struck at all the Bisbee-Warren mines. Since Bisbee-Warren was the leading copper producing area in the nation, the strike had the potential of hurting the war effort. Superficial evidence supported the belief that this was the intent of the strike. First, the IWW was a socialist organization. As such, it employed anti-nationalist rhetoric, and its official doctrine opposed war. Second, about half of the IWW strikers were aliens including not only a good many from Mexico recently displaced by the revolution, but also a significant number from Austria-Hungary. Mexicans and Mexican Americans were generally suspected of harboring a pro-German bias because of the friction on the border and the British discovery of the Zimmerman note by which Germany had planned to induce Mexico into war against the United States. The Bisbee-Warren mines had traditionally employed a large number of British citizens, "Cousin Johns from Cornwall." With the outbreak of the war, many of this supposedly loyal work force left to join the British military. Yet the number of British citizens among the IWW strikers was approximately the same as the number of Austro-Hungarians and there were almost no Germans. So to say that the strikers were pro-German is suspect unless a large number of the British nationals were Irish.

Miners' unions had struggled for years for recognition in the copper industry of Southern Arizona, and management violently opposed them. The reader should recall the Morenci strike and strikes in Bisbee mentioned earlier. This evidence suggests that mine operators, perhaps on a subconscious level at least, saw the war as an opportunity to roll back the advances made in recent years by the unions. At the very least, mine operators did not want to deal with a strike when profits were reaching an all-time high during a temporary war boom.

John C. Greenway, an ardent nationalist, succumbed to war hysteria and anti-alien propaganda spewed by many, but particularly by Theodore Roosevelt. But even in calmer times, Greenway had no use for unions. He sincerely believed in industrial paternalism, and he had made it work well in Minnesota where he supervised the construction of company towns which were clean and safe and contributed to the workers' well-being with good schools, libraries, and recreational facilities. To Greenway, when the IWW struck in 1917, these workers were being disloyal to the companies and to the nation. He was reinforced in this opinion by the knowledge that "Bisbee mines pay the highest wages of any copper camp in the United States" (Greenway's own words).

In earlier western strikes, mine operators had requested National Guard or federal troops ostensibly to protect life and property but actually to end strikes quickly. One might expect that during a major war this ploy should work well. However, in response to a request for federal troops by John Greenway, US Army Adjutant General McCain reported that an army colonel was sent to Bisbee and "no disturbance of any kind" was observed.

Unable to get assistance from either the state or federal government in ending the strike, mine operators, including Greenway, along with Sheriff Harry Wheeler, and some local citizens contrived a scheme to end the strike quickly. In the early morning of July 12, 1917, two thousand armed deputies under Wheeler's command rounded up known or suspected IWW strikers and marched them to a ball field where they were held until they could be loaded on to freight cars. The cars were sealed, and the strikers were taken without food or water across the state line to the desert near Columbus, New Mexico where they were released. Fortunately, they were rescued by federal troops who set up temporary camps for them. [62]

President Wilson ordered an investigation. The commission investigating the Bisbee affair was headed by a young Felix Frankfurter. They reported that the affair was "unprovoked and unjustified" and "wholly illegal…without authority of law, either State or Federal." The commission even asserted that the deportation was actually harmful to the war effort. The incident has since been heavily researched by many scholars, and as late as 1982, James W. Byrkit could write in Forging the Copper Collar that "no evidence has ever been produced that anyone other than the company goons, vigilantes, deputies, soldiers and police used violence…." The reaction of Roosevelt to the commission's report seems shocking. The ex-president wrote a scathing letter to Frankfurter, calling the attitude reflected in the commission's report "fundamentally that of Trotsky and the other Bolsheviki leaders of Russia." "Your report," he continued, "is as thoroughly misleading a document as could be written on the subject…. No human being in his senses doubts that the men deported from Bisbee were bent on destruction and murder." In Roosevelt's world of absolutes, the evil rhetoric of the IWW made that organization absolutely evil. Roosevelt often spoke sympathetically about organized labor, but he meant the tame labor unions of the East with gentlemen leaders like his friend, John Mitchell. He was, no doubt, pleased that Bisbee now had no union. In his mind that was better than the un-American, socialist IWW.

---

62 Sheriff Wheeler is the same Harry Wheeler who, as captain of the Arizona Rangers, had won praise from the unions in Bisbee for his impartiality in an earlier Bisbee strike. Wheeler, incidentally, had had some aspirations to run for governor before this famous Bisbee "deportation" incident, but he felt that his chances had been ruined by the bad publicity which resulted.

Many of the deported workers sued the copper companies. All these suits were settled out of court. Criminal charges were also filed. John Greenway was among many prominent Bisbee citizens actually arrested and charged with violating the strikers' civil rights. That case dragged on through appeals.

Before the case was settled, Greenway had sailed to France as a major in the US Army corps of engineers. En route he had prepared a will which included $100,000 to the miners of the New Cornelia Mine of Ajo, Arizona. Greenway's service in the war was extraordinary. He won the Distinguished Service Cross for "extraordinary heroism." He also won the Legion of Honor and the Croix de Guerre, and the Croix de l'Etoile Noire for "bravery and meritorious service" from France. His rank on release from military service was brigadier general. By the time he returned to Arizona all charges against him had been dropped. The Supreme Court of the United States had ruled that the federal government had no authority to bring charges and the state of Arizona was reluctant to pursue that affair. For his part, Greenway, like Roosevelt, remained certain that the deportation was justified and that the strike had been part of a pro-German conspiracy.

Only a few of the other Rough Riders enlisted for the Great War. First Sergeant William Davidson had an extraordinary career. He had fallen very ill with fever in Cuba. His condition was reported as "very serious" as he was at one time "semicomatose." Yet he survived, regained his health, and after age fifty re-enlisted in the army to serve in this next war. Greenway mentioned casually in one letter to another Rough Rider that Davidson had served with him in Europe and had been wounded but had recovered. David Goodrich, president of Goodrich Rubber Company and a New York Rough Rider, also saw combat in Europe. He rose to the rank of Lieutenant Colonel. George Wilcox answered the call of 1917, was commissioned a major, and did riot duty in Winston-Salem.

Immediately following the war, he volunteered as a local president of the Home Services Department of the American Red Cross. Mrs. George McCabe was secretary of that organization. Dan Hogan of Flagstaff commanded a company of the home guard and served on a civil defense committee. J. L. B. Alexander served as chairman of the draft exemption board in Phoenix.

Theodore Roosevelt had been an early advocate of military preparedness and a staunch supporter of war. Denied the opportunity to serve himself, he sent four sons into the melee. Unlike the short, romantic, adventurous war of 1898, this European war was a blood bath. The horror became vividly real and personal to Theodore and Edith Roosevelt when they learned of the death of their youngest son, Quentin. The old colonel wrote privately to his daughter that, "There is no use making believe that this death is other than a terrible and irretrievable calamity; nothing atones for it, but he has won a shining place as the embodiment in this war of spirit of service and sacrifice of the nation."

Roosevelt's own health was failing. His exploration of the River of Doubt in South America in early 1914 had nearly killed him. An injured leg abscessed, and he developed a severe jungle fever which contributed to his weakened condition thereafter. Now he had gout and rheumatism. He was deaf in one ear and blind in one eye.[63] He had been hospitalized for almost a month in February 1918, and he returned to the hospital on November 11, the day the armistice was signed. He died January 6, 1919 at home in his sleep. He was only sixty years old. Two days before his death, the ex-president had been visited by his old friend John Greenway who found him alert and lively in conversation. Alexander Brodie died later that same year. The age of the Rough Riders had passed.

---

63 Unknown to most people at the time, Roosevelt had been blind in one eye for many years, the result of a boxing match in the White House during his presidency.

CHAPTER 8

Some Conclusions

There was no doubt of the strong tie that bound the Rough Riders, as they were later called, together. We always teased my brother when, as President, he would suddenly announce the "Happy Jack of Arizonia," [sic] or some such erstwhile comrade, was eminently fitted for a position for which the aforesaid "Happy Jack" did not seem to have strong qualifications. How they loved their leader, and how that love was returned! Whenever my brother spoke of his "regiment" a note of tenderness came into his voice such as might be heard in the voice of a woman when speaking of her lover.

—Corrine Roosevelt

Most of Roosevelt's appointees in Arizona appear to have been reasonably well qualified. He did, however, ignore the convention of allowing party leaders in the territory to select most appointees, and he further alienated Republican Party leaders in Arizona by appointing some Democrats to coveted positions of patronage. This precedent breaking pattern of patronage distribution was not confined to Arizona. The strong preference for Rough Riders in appointive positions was also apparent in other southwestern territories, and this President crossed party lines to appoint Democrats in southeastern states where he observed that "there has really been no Republican Party, simply a set of black and white scalawags."

While other presidents before and since merely confirmed selections made by state (or territorial) party leaders, Theodore Roosevelt took his appointment duty very seriously. Prominent historian Henry Adams observed that Roosevelt seemed to be "devoured by small personal details" such as "appointments or removals of fourth-rate officials in remote mountains under cowboy influence." Roosevelt's hands-on leadership style did cause him to be occupied with more detail than other presidents, but his direct selection of top appointive officials also allowed him firm control in the territories without being directly involved in day-to-day affairs. He chose men he knew personally and trusted implicitly.

The close connection of both Governor Brodie and James McClintock with the President may have been an important factor in the selection of Arizona for the first major project under the Newlands Reclamation Act. The site of the project had been chosen by McClintock's party in 1890, and both McClintock and Brodie were long-term proponents of reclamation for central Arizona. Without the favor of the President, we can assume that Arizona Territory, with no representation in the Senate and only one non-voting member in the House, may not have been selected for a project which demanded such a considerable investment.

Alexander Brodie was one of the three Rough Rider governors appointed by Roosevelt in the territories. The other two were George Curry in New Mexico and Frank Frantz in Oklahoma. At the time of his appointment, the former Arizonan, Frantz, was the youngest governor in the United

States. While Brodie had always been a Republican, Curry and Frantz had both been Democrats.

As late as the 1904 election, George Curry said boldly in a newspaper interview, "I am a Democrat, have always been a Democrat, and couldn't be anything else if I tried." He also predicted that Roosevelt would be defeated for re-election. Roosevelt later picked Curry as New Mexico governor, despite Curry's political leanings. Having been out of the country at the time that a scandal implicating prominent New Mexicans had forced the previous governor from office, Curry was a safe choice for that territory's chief executive. In the last months of his presidency, Roosevelt could say with pride, "I'm awfully pleased with Curry."

Frantz, on the other hand, made a more rapid conversion to the Republican ranks on his return from the Cuban war, and quickly moved up the appointment lad-der under President Roosevelt, first as an Oklahoma postmaster, then Indian agent, and finally Oklahoma governor. Of the three governors, only Frantz was ever accused of any wrongdoing in office, and those accusations were politically motivated. (Frantz was a candidate to be Oklahoma's first state governor.) He was completely exonerated.

By appointing men in whom he had complete faith to top positions in the territories, President Roosevelt pro-vided the territories with efficient, honest government. The unique bond between the colonel and the men of the regiment also brought out the best qualities of honesty and service in those Rough Riders appointed to high office in Arizona. These men were as aware as the colonel of what he called "the double burden" to oneself "and to the regiment to make the best kind of record." They were, after all, the best of the Rough Riders in Arizona and those closest to Roosevelt. Conscious of the scrutiny given Rough Riders in Arizona, an obviously underpaid Governor Brodie refused supplemental allowances granted by the

—

territorial legislature after Roosevelt had warned him to be extremely careful with territorial funds as he took office.

No Rough Riders felt this double burden more than Ben Daniels. Roosevelt had risked his personal reputation a second time for Daniels after the lawman had once betrayed his confidence. Daniels met the challenge splendidly, and the record he made suggests the redemptive power of the faith of one human being in another. Of course, Daniels might have performed his duties just a well if he had received the appointment under different circumstances or from a different president. This was a different Ben Daniels from the Dodge City gunman. He was more mature, and he was more in the public eye with more to lose than before. The record he achieved in Arizona in the twentieth century cannot fully atone for a murder he committed in Kansas in the nineteenth, but the Arizona marshal did prove that the old Ben Daniels had been left in the preceding century.

The three other Rough Riders who held prominent positions in Arizona and also performed their duties honorably and efficiently are US Attorney J. L. B. Alexander, Arizona Ranger Captain (and later Prison Superintendent) Thomas Rynning, and Collector of Revenue for Arizona and New Mexico Henry Bardshar.

The negative side to Roosevelt's tendency to appoint only like-minded men who were fiercely loyal was that a group-think mentality evolved stifling any questioning of Roosevelt's policies. Consequently, these men, who might have contributed valuable advice on regional issues, acted only as operatives. Governor Brodie did break with the President over jointure. However, even on this issue which was repugnant to ninety percent of Arizonans, Ben Daniels and George Wilcox stood with the President. Tom Rynning said in his book that Wilcox and other Rough Riders had admonished him for not supporting Roosevelt on the jointure issue as a matter of loyalty.

—

Loyalty to the President prevented officials from suggesting creative, desirable alternatives. Certainly America's policies regarding the Yaqui fight in Mexico might have been rethought. The Roosevelt administration's whole relationship to the Diaz government, for that matter, seems to have been based on some fundamental misunderstandings. And both Marshal Daniels and US Attorney Alexander used a considerable portion of their resources to reduce the flow of illegal Chinese immigrants through Mexico, resources which might have been better used on more important projects. The tendency to discourage meaningful dialogue and alternatives was the greatest weakness of Roosevelt's leadership.

The negative effects of group think were manifest in the way policies were carried out. As the involvement of America in Mexico's looming revolution concerned Roosevelt, suppression of Mexican revolutionaries north of the border became a priority of Arizona law enforcement. This led to overzealous efforts by Marshal Daniels and Ranger Captain Rynning. US Attorney Alexander vigorously prosecuted Mexican dissidents, but also recommended merciful sentencing on occasion.

The dearth of patronage under Roosevelt demoralized the Republican Party in the territory. Party discipline suffered as Roosevelt appointees felt no need to contribute to the party coffers, while party regulars were often denied reasonable rewards for party service. The election of a more traditional Republican president, William Howard Taft, and a Republican congressional delegate for Arizona in 1908 meant a return to traditional methods of allotting patronage. This surprised some Roosevelt appointees in the territory who naively assumed that their jobs were secure. Three of the Rough Rider appointees played key roles in Arizona's short lived Progressive Party. These men were J. L. B. Alexander, George Wilcox, and Ben Daniels. Each of these men had protested his own removal. All three were former Democrats who had not contributed money to the party. James McClintock, on the other hand, kept his job as Phoenix postmaster with the change of administrations. He, in sharp contrast to the others aforementioned, was a long time Republican who was active in the party.

Rough Rider John Greenway joined Alexander, Wilcox, and Daniels, and Dwight Heard to form the nucleus of the leadership of the Arizona Progressives. The four Rough Riders were fiercely loyal to Roosevelt. Heard, too, was a friend of the colonel. We can also assume that the bitterness that Alexander, Wilcox, and Daniels felt at their dismissals contributed to their zeal in opposing the Republican Party in 1912. Other Rough Riders were active in the Progressive campaign of 1912 at lower levels. Notable among these are Richard Stanton, who had been turned down by the Republican Party in his bid to replace Daniels as marshal, and Charles Utting, a former deputy under Daniels.

Heard is the only member among these leaders who showed a long term commitment to the Progressive Party. He purchased the *Arizona Republican* so that it could be the clarion of the Progressive doctrine. For the four Rough Riders who joined him in leading the 1912 campaign, Progressivism was not a lasting passion. All returned to the Republican camp by the time of the 1916 general election. Daniels ran for sheriff of Pima County on the Republican ticket that year. After officially wishing Republican presidential candidate Charles Evens Hughes success, Alexander disbanded the Arizona Progressive Party and contributed a small sum to the Republican Party. George Wilcox had also grown in his understanding of political reality. He soon proclaimed himself an "active Republican, deeply interested in the success and welfare of his party." Greenway was the least enthusiastic about the GOP and for most of the rest of his life straddled the fence between both major parties, but in 1916 he was selected as a

Republican Party elector and would, therefore, have cast a vote for Hughes if he had won Arizona.

This work, I believe, clearly shatters the persistent myth that the Arizona Rangers were dominated by former Rough Riders. The Rough Riders were in no way dominant among the Rangers, and Captain Rynning did not show a strong preference for his former comrades in his hiring policies. As has been shown, only seven Rough Riders served under the three Ranger captains. Three of those seven were hired by Burton Mossman, the first Ranger captain who had only thirteen men under him. Only one Rough Rider, other than Rynning himself, served more than one year in the Rangers, and only two Rough Riders were promoted beyond the rank of private.

Having risen to the pinnacle of American politics through his command of the Rough Riders, Roosevelt continued to benefit politically from his position as honorary permanent president of the "Roosevelt Rough Rider Association." Three of the four reunions in which "the colonel" participated increased his political capital. The 1899 reunion in Las Cruces, New Mexico, refocused attention on his war record when it might have soon been forgotten while providing him with an excuse to leave New York and make a national tour. The second (1900) reunion in Oklahoma City again brought attention to his status as a war hero at the beginning of his campaign for the vice-presidency. The third (1901) reunion in Colorado Springs presented potential political pitfalls, but careful management avoided problems. At the Colorado Springs reunion, Roosevelt convinced the Association's members to abandon annual reunions in favor of one every four years. When the next reunion was held in San Antonio in 1905, Roosevelt was given such a hearty welcome in Texas that he soon planned a tour of the old Confederacy, where he may have envisioned the Republican Party had a chance of becoming viable.

Perhaps the most interesting and revealing personal relationship included in this work is that between Theodore Roosevelt and Benjamin Daniels. Two factors explain Roosevelt's unusual confidence in Daniels. First, Roosevelt was convinced by Daniels' service in Cuba that, regardless of his past, the former Dodge City deputy was now essentially honest and dependable, or, at the very least, that Daniels, once in office, would perform his duties in such a way as to be certain not to again embarrass his old colonel. Secondly, based on his own experience ranching in Dakota Territory, Roosevelt viewed the old west of the late nineteenth century as the "Viking age" in America. He used this term in at least two letters and in his autobiography. In this bygone age, men occasionally fought and killed each other with guns in what Roosevelt perceived as the normal course of events. The law was crude and men could commonly be on both sides of it at different times. With this belief, Roosevelt had convinced himself that Daniels' actions in this "Viking age" were probably not unusual. The violent nature of these "Vikings" was, after all, part of what made them good soldiers in Cuba.

Lastly, what must be noted is that a Rough Rider network did provide lower level government jobs in Arizona. Both President Roosevelt and Governor Brodie tried to accommodate their office seeking comrades.

Many former Rough Riders served as guards at the territorial prison and some did become postmasters, but Rough Riders seem to have received no particular preferential hiring as Arizona Rangers and little or none as deputy marshals. Much of the patronage came from Brodie rather than Roosevelt.

Toward the end of *The Rough Riders* Roosevelt focused on these characteristics of his men which made many good leaders:

The difference as regards officers and non-commissioned officers, between regular and volunteers, is usually very great; but in my regiment (keeping in view the material we had to handle), it was easy to develop non-commissioned officers out of men who had been round-up foremen, ranch foremen, mining bosses, and the like. These men were intelligent and resolute; they knew they had a great deal to learn, and they set to work learning it; while they were already accustomed to managing considerable interests, to obeying orders, and to taking care of others as well as themselves.

In many of his Rough Rider appointments, especially at higher levels, President Roosevelt acted in the best interest of his own presidency and the country. In general, and with few minor exceptions, Roosevelt's Rough Riders performed their duties well in various appointed positions and contributed positively to sound government in Arizona. At the highest levels, the colonel appointed men upon whom he could depend. Those men, in turn, acted not only with honor, but also with special care derived from the concern that they could bring either honor or dishonor on their regiment and their leader whom they loved.

Epilogue

With the dreams of a new party dashed and their leader dead, most Roosevelt backers returned, however reluctantly, to the Republican Party. John Greenway and fellow Rough Rider, George McCabe, also of Bisbee-Warren, supported Roosevelt surrogate, Leonard Wood, for the Republican presidential nomination in 1920. Benjamin Daniels, running as a Republican, was elected sheriff of Pima County that year. In his long law enforcement career this was his only elected position. Two years later in 1922, he was defeated in the Republican primary election. A letter he wrote to John Greenway shows that the lame duck sheriff had grown in political sophistication and may also have mellowed with age. He said that he was not upset by his defeat and he intended to support the candidate who had defeated him.

Greenway was himself unsuccessful in his political aspirations in 1922, as was fellow Rough Rider James McClintock. Greenway sought the Democratic nomination for governor. He led on the first twelve ballots at the state convention but finally withdrew to break a deadlock. McClintock actually obtained the Republican nomination for United States Senate, but he was defeated in the general election.

Greenway promoted the development of dams on the Colorado River, as he became increasingly active in the Democratic Party. He attended a 1923 interstate conference on development of the Colorado River. In 1924, as a delegate to the Democratic National Convention, he was honored with a nomination for vice president by his fellow Arizonans. The nomination was seconded by a delegate from Minnesota, where Greenway had planned and developed the model mining town of Coleraine in the best tradition of industrial paternalism.

At this time John Greenway's private life was as rewarding as his public life. He married in 1923 at the age of fifty-one to Isabella Ferguson, the widow of his old friend and Rough Rider comrade, Robert Ferguson. A year later a son, John Jr., was born. The following year he retired from his job as mine manager but continued his political activities in support of reclamation. Then in November 1925, while on a trip east to win support for a dam project, he suddenly became ill. Though he recovered quickly, his brother-in-law, Dr. W. L. Keller, diagnosed the illness as caused by a gall bladder problem which would require routine surgery. After getting a second opinion, Greenway scheduled the procedure for January 15, 1926. It was performed successfully, but a blood clot developed. Four days later John Greenway died. Like his colonel, he had lived life to the fullest right up to the end then died suddenly and young.

His funeral was an elaborate affair. Three thousand mourners converged on the small town of Ajo, Arizona where Greenway had developed the huge open-pit New Cornelia mine. Numerous veterans of both the Spanish-American War and the Great War attended including, of course, many former Rough Rider colleagues. A military plane came in low over the coffin; the pilot switched off the engine; and red and white carnations were dropped on the casket and the crowd. The grave was marked by a copper plate and a large boulder of copper ore. According to the Ajo *Copper News*, "The funeral of Gen. John C. Greenway at Ajo Jan. 26 has never been surpassed in the history of the State, in number of those attending; never duplicated in its drawing from all walks of life; unparalleled in its nearness to nature...." For many years, a daily flag raising at the site was observed, but that was discontinued long ago.

Sadly, today the grave site is in a state of disrepair and has been vandalized.

Arizona honored Greenway one more time a few years later. He was chosen as one of only two Arizonans to have a statue in his likeness exhibited in the National Statuary in Washington, DC. Gutzon Borglum, the sculptor of Mount Rushmore, designed the likeness with the consultation of Isabella Greenway, John's widow, who had gone on to become Arizona's first female representative to Congress. After one long meeting with Borglum in San Antonio, Mrs. Greenway beamed with enthusiasm. She reported back in Arizona that, "He wouldn't let me leave until I had told him my husband's entire life story. After that he studied the photographs and examined the clothing of General Greenway that I had brought. He seemed to develop the most amazing insight into the character of the General. I know Mr. Borglum will make a wonderful statue."

The figure which Borglum created has a strength and calmness to it at the same time. It makes an interesting contrast to Arizona's other occupant of the National Statuary, the likeness of Father Eusebio Kino. The Kino statue exhibits calm with a glowing inner strength. The two, both beautifully crafted, complement each other and seem to belong together. Besides standing together in the National Statuary, duplicates of these stand at each end of the entrance to the Arizona Pioneers' Historical Society building in Tucson, Arizona. However, the Greenway statue in the National Statuary has been replaced by one of Barry Goldwater.

Of course, the most famous Rough Rider statue is that of Buckey O'Neill by Solon Borglum in Prescott. It is the centerpiece for a city alive with the memory of O'Neill. Among the businesses which surround the town square are Bucky O'Neill Sporting Goods, Bucky's Bean Bag, and Bucky's Sandwich Emporium. A little farther out on state route 69 one can find Bucky's Casino, an establishment which is a truly fitting tribute to the man who earned his nickname by his frequent willingness to gamble his last dollar with good natured, reckless abandon.

James McClintock died in 1934. In addition to his service as postmaster of Phoenix, commander of the Arizona National Guard, and Republican Party Committeeman, McClintock had also served as official state historian from 1919 to 1922. His contributions to the writing of Arizona history include a useful three volume history of Arizona, as well as a short history of the Mormon pioneers of Arizona. J. L. B. Alexander, the third Arizona Rough Rider captain, preceded McClintock in death three years earlier. Both McClintock and Alexander had been very active in the Spanish War Veterans Association, and Alexander's second wife, Grace, remained active and prominent in the auxiliary, serving as national president in 1949–50.

A fiftieth year Rough Rider reunion was organized in Prescott in 1948 and was a huge success. Approximately seventy of the estimated one hundred sixty surviving Rough Riders attended, and the members agreed to hold annual reunions in Prescott to coincide with the July 4 rodeo beginning the following year.

The long-time Rough Rider survivors should be mentioned here. Daniel Hogan, the oldest of the Flagstaff recruits, was the last survivor of that group. He died in 1957 at the age of ninety. George Wilcox died two months short his eighty-sixth birthday in 1949. According to his son, he was alert and active to the end and had attended a Rough Rider reunion the week before his death. Arthur Tuttle was the last surviving Arizona Rough Rider. He died in Salinas, California in 1969. He too retained his mental capacity to the end and was, in the words of author Charles Herner, "a living link with the" now distant "past."

As for Roosevelt, his bid for the Medal of Honor was reconsidered over a century later. In November 1998 President Clinton at the urging of Congress directed the army to investigate the actions of Theodore Roosevelt on July 1, 1898, for the purpose of evaluating whether the colonel should now receive the Medal of Honor. The medal was granted in early 2001. Roosevelt was disappointed by being denied the medal during his lifetime, but undoubtedly, he was consoled by his own conviction that he had proven his courage in battle. The instant popularity which he gained made July 1, 1898, the turning point in his life.

Notes on the Sources

Most of the information in the book comes from unpublished collections available at the three Arizona state universities, the Arizona Historical Society Pioneer Museum (Tucson), Arizona Historical Foundation (Tempe), the Sharlot Hall Museum (Prescott) and the Phoenix Public Library. The complete collection of the letters of Theodore Roosevelt has also been used extensively. They are available at the Library of Congress and on microfilm at the University of Arizona. *The Letters of Theodore Roosevelt* edited by Elting Morison are also available in an abridged collection of eight volumes. Many of the prolific writings of Roosevelt, himself, have also been useful in this work. Obvious sources include *The Rough Riders* and Roosevelt's autobiography. *The Winning of the West*, Roosevelt's famous six volume classic, was valuable for what it says about its author's views.

With the recent one hundredth anniversary of the Spanish-American War, several new books have been written about this episode in American history and Colonel Roosevelt's famous regiment. Prominent among these are Dale Walker's *The Boys of '98* (1998), David Traxel's *1898: The Birth of the American Century* (1998), Ivan Musicant's *Empire by Default* (1998), H. Paul Jeffer's *Colonel Roosevelt* (1996), and *Teddy Roosevelt at San Juan* by Peggy and Harold Samuels (1997). *Rough Writings* (1998), a brief anthology edited by Janet Lovelady and published by the Sharlot Hall Museum contains some primary material, including letters home written by Arizona Rough Rider Lieutenant Joshua Carter.

Books written about Roosevelt are numerous. Two major Roosevelt biographies were published in the 1990s. These are *Theodore Roosevelt: A Life* by Nathan Miller (1992) and *TR: The Last Romantic* by H.W. Brands (1997). Two other less ambitious works which have been recently published are also interesting. These are *The Lion's Pride: Theodore Roosevelt and His Family in Peace and War* by Edward J. Renehan, Jr., (1998) and *Carry a Big Stick: The Uncommon Heroism of Theodore Roosevelt* (1996) by George Grant. Among the classic Roosevelt biographies worth reading are Edmund Morris' *The Rise of Theodore Roosevelt* and Henry F. Pringle's *Theodore Roosevelt*. For Roosevelt as a leader of the Progressive Party, John Allen Gable's *The Bull Moose Years* and George Mowry's *Theodore Roosevelt and the Progressive Movement* are both worth reading.

Two good but older secondary books are available dealing specifically with the Rough Riders. Directly related to this work and an excellent source Charles Herner's *The Arizona Rough Riders*. Virgil Carrington Jones deals with the entire regiment in his classic work, *Roosevelt's Rough Riders*. Books written by the Rough Riders and their associates are few and generally flawed. Roosevelt's own Rough Rider book was written in haste and can be criticized for many minor errors, but it is an important source for the colonel's feelings toward various individuals in the regiment. Tom Hall, one-time regimental adjutant, also wrote a book, which he titled *The Fun and Fighting of the Rough Riders*. It is anecdotal and limited in scope. Richard Harding Davis, a reporter who attached himself to the regiment, is admiring and uncritical when he mentions the Rough Riders in his books *The Notes of a War Correspondent* and *The Cuban and Porto (sic) Rican Campaigns*. The same is true for *The Story of the Rough Riders* by Davis' fellow correspondent Edward Marshall. Marshall's work, however, makes use of interviews with former Rough Riders after the war in addition to Marshall's own observations.

Joseph Wheeler's *The Santiago Campaign* is reliable but limited in its information about the Rough Riders. Wheeler was the commander of all cavalry in Cuba.

The only three individual Rough Riders about whom biographies have been published at this time are Captain William "Buckey" O'Neill, Lieutenant Tom Harbo Rynning, and Lieutenant John C. Greenway. Two books have been written about O'Neill. They are *Buckey O'Neill* by Ralph Keithley (1949) and *Death was the Black Horse* by Dale Walker (1975). The latter has been reprinted as *Rough Rider: Buckey O'Neill of Arizona* (1997). Tom Rynning's autobiography as told to Al Cohn and Joe Chisolm is entitled *Gun Notches*. Though this book has a somewhat self-serving tone throughout, it contains some useful information. John Greenway, who relocated to Arizona in 1910, is the subject of a biography emphasizing his work in the iron producing region of northeastern Minnesota entitled *John Greenway and the Opening of the Western Mesabi* (1975).

James McClintock's own *Arizona: Prehistoric-Aboriginal-Pioneer-Modern* is a three-volume general history of the state. It is an important primary source of information related to the Rough Riders and this time period of Arizona history. A far better history of the territorial days, however, is Jay J. Wagoner's *Arizona Territory 1863–1912*. Another good popular history of Arizona is *Arizona, A Cavalcade of History* by Marshall Trimble.

Bibliography

I. Unpublished Sources

Collection of James Harvey McClintock. Phoenix Public Library, Phoenix, Arizona.

Collection of McClintock-Halseth. Arizona Historical Foundation, Hayden Library, Arizona State University, Tempe, Arizona.

Hill, Charles Douglas. "The Arizona Rangers: Frontier Law and Order in the Twentieth Century." Master's thesis, Arizona State University, 1977.

Hughes, David L. "A Story of the Rough Riders." Unpublished manuscript, Arizona Pioneers' Historical Society, Tucson, Arizona.

Hunter, George. "John C. Greenway and the Bull Moose Movement in Arizona." Master's thesis, University of Arizona, 1966.

McClintock, James Harvey, *Forward Arizona*, transcripts of broadcasts over KTAR radio, 1931, Arizona Pioneers' Historical Society, Tucson. No. 45 "Arizona in the Cuban War." No. 46 "Organization of the Rough Riders." No. 47 "The Arizona Rough Riders in Cuba." No. 48 "Arizona's Citizen Soldiers."

Kittell, Larry Waite. "The Administration of Alexander O. Brodie, Arizona Territorial Governor, 1902–1905." Master's thesis, University of Arizona, 1973.

Papers of Joseph L. B. and Grace Alexander. Special collections, Arizona State University, Tempe, Arizona.

Papers of Ralph H. Cameron. Special collections, University of Arizona, Tucson, Arizona.

Papers of Benjamin Franklin Daniels. Arizona Pioneers' Historical Society, Tucson, Arizona.

Papers of John Campbell Greenway. Arizona Historical Society Pioneer Museum, Tucson, Arizona.

Papers of Emilio Kosterlitzky. Special collections, University of Arizona, Tucson, Arizona.

Papers of Theodore Roosevelt. National Archives, Washington, DC. (Copies on microfilm at the University of Arizona, Tucson.)

Papers of George Smalley. Arizona Pioneers' Historical Society, Tucson, Arizona.

Papers of George Truman, Arizona Pioneers' Historical Society, Tucson, Arizona.

Probst, Avan S. "Isabella Greenway: Arizona's 1933 Congresswoman." Master's thesis, Northern Arizona University, 1994.

"Spanish War Scrapbook." Sharlot Hall Museum, Prescott, Arizona.

Wilson, Roscoe. "Roscoe Wilson Scrapbook." Sharlot Hall Museum, Prescott, Arizona.

II. Newspapers

Argus, (Holbrook, Arizona)

Arizona Republican, (Phoenix)

Arizona Journal-Miner, (Prescott)

Arizona Silver Belt, (Globe)

Copper News, (Ajo, Arizona)

Democrat, (Dodge City, Kansas)

Globe Livestock, (Dodge City, Kansas)

New York Times

Prospector, (Tombstone, Arizona)

Daily Citizen, (Tucson)

III. Public Documents

Appointment Papers of Benjamin F. Daniels. National Archives, Washington, DC.

Appointment and Reappointment Papers of Joseph L.B. Alexander. National Archives, Washington, DC.

Arizona United States Marshal's Papers. Arizona Pioneers' Historical Society, Tucson, Arizona.

"Bisbee Deportation," United States Justice files, Special collections, Northern Arizona University, Flagstaff, Arizona.

Personnel files of the Arizona Rangers. Arizona Historical Foundation, Hayden Library, Arizona State University, Tempe, Arizona.

Prisoner Description Record of the United States Penitentiary at Laramie City, Wyoming. Number 86, November 29, 1879.

IV. Published Primary Materials

Brodie, Alexander O. "Reclaiming the Arid Southwest," *Cosmopolitan*, vol. 37, no. 6, October 1904, pp. 715–722.

Foner, Philip S. ed. *Mother Jones Speaks: Collected Writings and Speeches*, New York: Monad Press, 1983.

McClintock, James Harvey. *Arizona: Prehistoric-Aboriginal-Pioneer-Modern*, 3 volumes. Chicago: The S. J. Clark Publishing Company, 1916.

Morison, Elting E. ed. *The Letters of Theodore Roosevelt*, 8 volumes. Cambridge: Harvard University Press, 1951.

Robinson, Corrine Roosevelt. *My Brother Theodore Roosevelt*. New York: Charles Scribner's Sons, 1922.

Roosevelt, Theodore. "Arizona and the Recall of the Judiciary," *The Outlook*, vol. 98 (June 24, 1911) pp. 378–379.

______. *Pocket Dairy, 1898: Theodore Roosevelt's Private Account of the War with Spain*, ed. Wallace Finley Daily. Cambridge: The President and Fellows of Harvard College, 1998.

______. *The Rough Riders*. New York: Review of Reviews, 1899.

______. *Theodore Roosevelt, an Autobiography*. New York: Charles Scribner's Sons, 1926.

______. *The Winning of the West*, 6 volumes. New York: Charles Scribner's Sons, 1889.

Roosevelt, Theodore and Henry Cabot Lodge. *Selections from the Correspondences of Theodore Roosevelt and Henry Cabot Lodge, 1884–1918*, 2 volumes. New York: Charles Scribner's Sons, 1925.

Rynning, Thomas H. *Gun Notches: The Life Story of a Cowboy-Soldier* as told to Al Cohn and Joe Chisolm. New York: A.L. Burt Company Publisher, 1931.

Sloan, Richard E. *Memories of an Arizona Judge*. Palo Alto: Stanford University Press, 1932.

Smalley, George Herbert. *My Adventures in Arizona: Leaves from a Reporter's Notebook*, edited by Yndia Smalley Moore. Tucson: Arizona Pioneers' Historical Society, 1966.

Wheeler, Joseph. *The Santiago Campaign, 1898*. Boston: Lamson, Wolfe and Company, 1898.

V. Secondary Materials

Ball, Larry D. *United Sates Marshals of New Mexico and Arizona Territories, 1846–1912*. Albuquerque: University of New Mexico Press, 1978.

Boese, Donald L. *John C. Greenway and the Opening of the Western Mesabi*. Grand Rapids, Minnesota: Itasca Community College Foundation, 1975.

Bowers, Claude G. *Beveridge and the Progressive Era*. New York: The Literary Guide, 1932.

Braeman, John. *Albert Beveridge: American Nationalist*. Chicago: The University of Chicago Press, 1982.

Brands, H.W. *TR: The Last Romantic*. New York: Basic Books, 1997.

Byrkit, James W. *Forging the Copper Collar: Arizona's Labor-Management War of 1901–1921*. Tucson: The University of Arizona Press, 1982.

Chessman, G. Wallace. *Governor Theodore Roosevelt: The Albany Apprenticeship*, Cambridge: Harvard University Press, 1965.

Cline, Platt. *Mountain Town: Flagstaff's First Century*. Flagstaff, Arizona: Northland Press, 1994.

De Arment, Robert. "County Seat War," *True West* (Sept.–Oct. 1967) pp. 20–22.

Dill, David B. Jr. "Terror on the Hassayampa: The Walnut Grove Dam Disaster of 1890," *The Journal of Arizona History*, vol. 28, no. 3 (Autumn 1987) pp. 283–290.

Dubofsky, Melvyn. *We Shall Be All: A History of the Industrial Workers of the World*, second edition. Chicago: University of Illinois Press, 1988.

Fethering, Dale. *Mother Jones, the Miners' Angel: A Portrait*. Carbondale, IL: Southern Illinois University Press, 1974.

Fireman, Bert M. *Arizona: Historic Land*. New York: Alfred A. Knopf, 1982.

Gable, John Allen. *The Bull Moose Years: Theodore Roosevelt and the Progressive Party*. Port Washington, New York: Kennikat Press, 1978.

Goff, John S. *George W. P. Hunt and His Arizona*. Pasadena: Socio-Technical Publications, 1973.

Harbaugh, William H. *The Life and Times of Theodore Roosevelt*. London: Oxford University Press, 1975.

Herner, Charles. *The Arizona Rough Riders*. Tucson: The University of Arizona Press, 1970.

Hunter, George S. "The Bull Moose Movement in Arizona," *Arizona and the West*, 10 (Winter 1968) pp. 343–362.

Hutton, Paul Andrew. "T. R. Takes Charge," *American History*, vol. 33, no. 3 (August 1998) pp. 33–38, 64–65.

Kelley, George H. *Legislative History: Arizona, 1864–1912*. Phoenix: George Kelley, Arizona State Historian.

Jeffers, H. Paul. *Colonel Roosevelt: Theodore Roosevelt Goes to War, 1897–1898*. New York: John Wiley & Sons, Inc., 1996.

Jensen, Vernon H. *Heritage of Conflict: Labor Relations in the Nonferrous Metal Industry up to 1930*. New York: Greenwood Press, 1968.

Jones, Virgil Carrington. *Roosevelt's Rough Riders*. Garden City: Doubleday & Company, Inc., 1971.

Lovelady, Janet, ed. *Rough Writings: Perspectives on Buckey O'Neill, Pauline M. O'Neill, and Roosevelt's Rough Riderts*. Prescott, Arizona: Sharlot Hall Museum Press, 1998.

Mangelsdorf, Karen Underhill. "The Beveridge Visit to Arizona in 1902," *The Journal of Arizona History*, vol. 28, no. 3 (Autumn 1987) pp. 243–260.

Marshall, Edward. *The Rough Riders*. New York: G. W. Dillingham Co., 1899.

Miller, Joseph, ed. *The Arizona Rangers*. New York: Hastings House, 1972.

Miller, Nathan. *Theodore Roosevelt: A Life*. New York: Quill,

William Morrow, 1992.

Millis, Walter. *The Martial Spirit*. Chicago: Ivan R. Dee, Inc., 1989.

Morris, Edmund. *The Rise of Theodore Roosevelt*. New York: Coward, McCann, & Geoghegan, Inc., 1979.

Mowry, George E. *Theodore Roosevelt and the Progressive Movement*. New York: Hill and Wang, 1946.

Musicant, Ivan. *Empire by Default: The Spanish-American War and the Dawn of the American Century*. New York: Henry Holt and Company, 1998.

O'Neal, Bill. *The Arizona Rangers*. Austin: Eakins Press, 1987.

Parkman, I.H. "Hassayampa Dam Disaster—1890," *Desert Magazine*, (November 1955) vol. 18, pp. 11–12.

Philips, Edward Hake. "Teddy Roosevelt in West Texas," *West Texas Historical Association Year Book* (1980) vol. 56, pp. 58–67.

Portrait and Biographical Record of Arizona. Chicago: Chapman Publishing Co., 1911.

Price, Willadene. *Gutzon Borglum: Artist and Patriot*. New York: Rand McNally & Company, 1961.

Pringle, Henry F. *Theodore Roosevelt: A Biography*. New York: Harcourt Brace Janovich, 1956.

Raat, W. Dirk. *Revoltosos: Mexican Rebels in the United States, 1903–1923*. College Station, TX: Texas A&M Press, 1981.

Rayburn, John C. "The Rough Riders in San Antonio, 1898," *Arizona and the West*, vol. 3, no. 2 (Summer 1961) pp. 113–128.

Renehan, Edward J., Jr. *The Lion's Pride: Theodore Roosevelt and His Family in Peace and War*. New York: Oxford University Press, 1998.

Samuels, Peggy and Harold Samuels. *Teddy Roosevelt at San Juan: The Making of a President*. College Station, TX: Texas A&M University Press, 1997.

Schwantes, Carlos A., ed. *Bisbee: Urban Outpost on the Frontier*. Tucson: University of Arizona Press, 1992.

Secrist, William. "Fighting Man," *Frontier Times* (April–May 1969) p. 6–13, 41–53.

Sell, Henry Backman and Victor Weybright. *Buffalo Bill and the Wild West*. New York: Oxford University Press, 1955.

Shirley, Glen. "Cap. Mossman and the Apache Devil." *True West*, (May 1957) pp. 4–6, 32–34.

Smith, Cornelius. *Emilio Kosterlitzky: Eagle of Sonora and the Southwest Border*. Glendale, CA: The Arthur H. Clark Company, 1970.

Smith, Karen L. *The Magnificent Experiment: Building the Salt River Reclamation Project, 1890–1917*. Tucson: University of Arizona Press, 1986.

Sonnichsen, C. L. *Colonel Green and the Copper Skyrocket*. Tucson: The University of Arizona Press, 1974.

The Taming of the Salt. Phoenix: Community Relations Department of the Salt River Project, 1970.

Traxel, David. *1898: The Birth of the American Century*. New York: Alfred A. Knopf, 1998.

Trimble, Marshall. *Arizona: A Cavalcade of History*. Tucson: Treasure Chest Publications, 1990.

Turner, John Kenneth. *Barbarous Mexico*. Austin: University of Texas Press, 1969.

Vanderwood, Paul J. and Frank N. Samponaro. *Border Fury: A Picture Postcard Record of Mexico's Revolution and US War Preparedness, 1910–1917*. Albuquerque: University of New Mexico Press, 1988.

Walker, Dale L. *The Boys of '98: Theodore Roosevelt and the Rough Riders*. New York: Tom Doherty Association, 1998.

_____. *Death was the Black Horse: The Story of Rough Rider Buckey O'Neill*. Austin: Madrova Press, 1970.

Wagoner, Jay J. *Arizona Territory 1863–1912: A Political History*. Tucson: The University of Arizona Press, 1970.

Woodward, Corner Vann. *Origins of the New South, 1877–1913*. Baton Rouge: Louisiana State University Press, 1951.

www.ingramcontent.com/pod-product-compliance
Lightning Source LLC
Chambersburg PA
CBHW022211050726
47590CB00002B/739